# Making Sense of English Grammar Exercises

Jake Allsop

CASSELL

CASSELL PUBLISHERS LIMITED
Artillery House, Artillery Row
London SW1P 1RT

© Cassell Publishers Limited 1989

All rights reserved. This book is protected by copyright. No part of it may be reproduced, stored in a retrieval system, or transmitted in any form or by any means, electronic, mechanical, photocopying, recording or otherwise, without written permission from the Publishers.

First published 1989

British Library Cataloguing in Publication Data

Allsop, Jake
   Making sense of English grammar exercises:
   self study edition (with answers)
   exercises for lower intermediate
   students
   1. English language — Text books for
   foreign speakers
   I. Title
   428.2'4   PE1128
   ISBN 0 304 31394 7

British Library Cataloguing in Publication Data

Allsop, Jake
   Making sense of English grammar exercises:
   exercises for lower intermediate
   students
   1. English language — Text books for
   foreign speakers
   I. Title
   428.2'4   PE1128
   ISBN 0 304 31403 X

Illustrations by Phillip Burrows
Design by Heather Richards
Typeset by Flairplan Ltd, Ware, Herts.
Printed in Great Britain by the Bath Press, Bath, Avon

# Contents

1 Nouns — 1
2 Determiners I — 6
3 Determiners II — 10
4 Determiners III — 13
5 Adjectivals — 16
6 Pronouns — 24
7 Prepositions — 28
8 Introduction to verbs — 33
9 Simple and continuous forms — 38
10 Perfect tenses — 43
11 The future — 46
12 Modals — 51
13 Conditionals — 55
14 The passive — 58
15 The imperative — 60
16 Gerund and infinitive — 63
17 Participles — 66
18 Phrasal verbs — 71
19 Adverbials — 74
20 Conjunctions — 79
21 Reported speech — 82

Answer key (*Self study edition* only) — 85

# Introduction

Exercises can be mechanical like, say, jogging; you may get fitter, but you can hardly say that you have had a good time.

Exercises can make you think, like, say, logic puzzles: you may enjoy yourself but you won't be any more intelligent afterwards.

Wouldn't it be nice to have a book of exercises which made you think, which were fun to do *and* which made you fitter, ie, better at English? That is what I have tried to provide.

The main chapters correspond to the chapters of *Making Sense of English Grammar* and contain over 50 short grammar summaries (marked with the symbol ▷) which come before each group of exercises. If you want fuller explanations, go to *Cassell's Students' English Grammar*. In most exercises you have to choose and manipulate English structures, so that you will understand and use them better. Several units have an exercise in which you are asked to see the difference between pairs of similar sentences.

This book will help you while you are spending time in the shallow end of the swimming pool. When you are ready to go swimming in the deeper water, try my more advanced book, *Cassell's Students' English Grammar Exercises*: it too has exercises to make you think, give you fun and – which is the main objective – make you fitter.

# 1 Nouns

▷ Nouns add *-s* or *-es* to form the plural: *dog – dogs, watch – watches*. Sometimes there is a spelling change: *wife – wives*. There are some special cases: *man – men*. Words ending in *-s/-es* are not always plural: *Mathematics is an easy subject*.

**1** Fill in the blanks with the correct singular or plural:

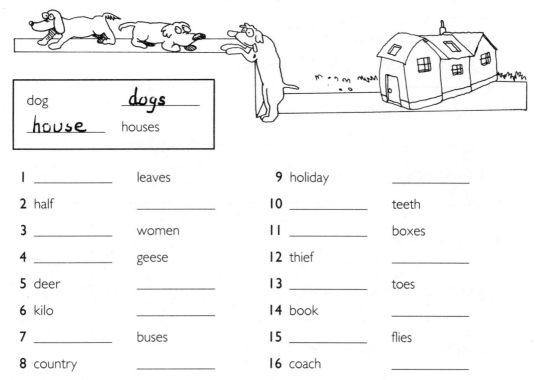

| dog | *dogs* |
| *house* | houses |

| 1 _____ | leaves | 9 holiday | _____ |
| 2 half | _____ | 10 _____ | teeth |
| 3 _____ | women | 11 _____ | boxes |
| 4 _____ | geese | 12 thief | _____ |
| 5 deer | _____ | 13 _____ | toes |
| 6 kilo | _____ | 14 book | _____ |
| 7 _____ | buses | 15 _____ | flies |
| 8 country | _____ | 16 coach | _____ |

**2** Fill in the blanks with the correct part of the verb:

| Your dinner ___*is*___ on the table. (*be*) |

1 The furniture we bought _____ not very expensive. (*be*)
2 The Chinese _____ very hardworking. (*be*)
3 _____ the red luggage belong to you? (*do*)
4 Your hair _____ very nice. (*look*)
5 _____ physics a difficult subject? (*be*)
6 The police _____ arrested several suspects. (*have*)
7 Your trousers _____ pressing. (*need*)

1

## 2–3 Nouns

8 Money _____ the world go round. (*make*)

9 I don't like people who _____ lies. (*tell*)

10 'No news _____ good news.' (*be*)

**3** Change the underlined words for the words in brackets and make any other changes necessary:

> There's a man in the garden. (*two*)
> **There are two men in the garden**

1 I need one tomato and half a potato. (*two/three*)

2 Knives are used to cut things. (*is*)

3 Is that your baby? (*those*)

4 Let's make a bookshelf. (*some*)

5 My tooth hurts: please take it out. (*them*)

6 This woman is a housewife. (*are*)

7 These are my grandchildren. (*is*)

8 Here is a photo of my daughter. (*some*)

9 There was a sheep in the garden. (*were*)

10 These shoes are too tight for my feet. (*This/foot*)

# Nouns 4–5

▷ Sometimes there is a different word for male and female: *brother – sister*. Usually the same word is used for male and female: *doctor*. Other words may tell you whether the person is male or female: *'Is <u>she</u> a doctor?'*

**4** Fill in the blanks:

| brother | **sister** |
| father | mother |

| | | | | |
|---|---|---|---|---|
| 1 nephew | _____ | 9 _____ | princess |
| 2 _____ | aunt | 10 master | _____ |
| 3 actor | _____ | 11 hero | _____ |
| 4 _____ | wife | 12 boyfriend | _____ |
| 5 grandson | _____ | 13 _____ | bride |
| 6 _____ | lady | 14 waiter | _____ |
| 7 _____ | widow | 15 bull | _____ |
| 8 policeman | _____ | 16 _____ | queen |

**5** Decide if the underlined item is male, female or not known, and put a cross in the right column:

| | Male | Female | Don't know |
|---|---|---|---|
| Is she a <u>doctor</u>? | | X | |
| Is he a <u>nurse</u>? | X | | |
| The <u>doctor</u> is busy. | | | X |
| 1 The <u>doctor</u> has left his car outside. | | | |
| 2 John's <u>driver</u> stayed at home because her mother was ill. | | | |
| 3 Is your <u>cousin</u> really an engineer? | | | |
| 4 The <u>boss</u> told her secretary to leave. | | | |
| 5 They left their <u>children</u> at home while they went shopping. | | | |
| 6 My niece is an <u>art teacher</u>. | | | |
| 7 The boss told his <u>secretary</u> to leave. | | | |
| 8 My <u>dog's</u> got no nose. How does he smell? | | | |
| 9 The <u>students</u> in this class work very hard. | | | |
| 10 My cousin Mary is married to an <u>accountant</u>. | | | |

## 6 Nouns

▷ The first part of a compound noun tells you something about the second part: a *bookshelf* is a *shelf* where you keep *books*.

**6** Complete the compound nouns from the list below:

**Nouns:** machine, watch, stick, booth, port, opener, driver, house, chair, office

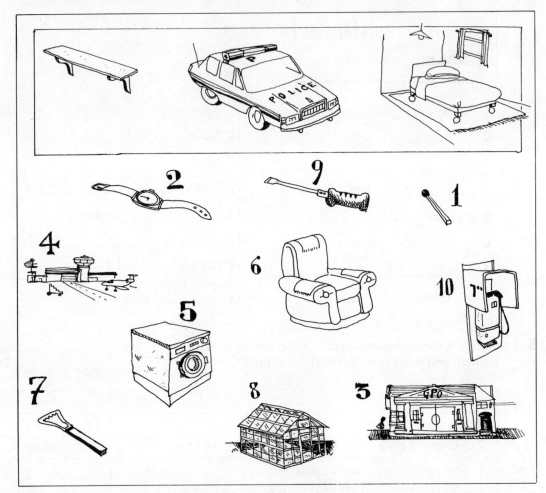

book **shelf**    police **car**    bed **room**

1 match _____    6 arm _____
2 wrist _____    7 bottle _____
3 post _____    8 green _____
4 air _____    9 screw _____
5 washing _____   10 telephone _____

# Nouns 7

▷ Use the possessive form -'s and -s' for people, animals, countries, and some expressions of place and time.

**7** Change the sentences below as shown:

> A holiday which lasts a week is __a week's holiday.__

1 The wages for three weeks are _____
2 The problems which we had yesterday are _____
3 A time three years from now is in _____ time.
4 A few minutes from now is in _____ time.

> Russia has an army. It is __Russia's army.__

5 These books belong to John. They are _____
6 The children sleep in this room. It is _____
7 The Smiths live here. This is _____ house.
8 Mr Jones is my boss. I am _____ secretary.
9 This room is for men only. It is _____
10 This study is for the girls. It is _____

> A butcher sells meat. We buy meat __at the butcher's.__

11 A greengrocer sells vegetables. We buy vegetables _____
12 An optician tests eyes. I got my eyes tested _____
13 A dentist looks after teeth. I must go _____
14 A chemist sells medicine. We buy medicine _____
15 Where do you buy bread? _____

# 2 Determiners 1
a/an and the; this/these and that/those

▷ *a* is used before a consonant sound; *an* is used before a vowel sound.

**1** Fill in the blanks with a suitable determiner:

> Give me **a** coke and **an** ice cream.

1 I'm wearing ___ yellow shirt and ___ orange tie.
2 ___ honest man is ___ happy man.
3 This is ___ easy exercise.
4 Is there ___ university in your town?
5 He is paid ___ pound ___ hour for his work.
6 ___ hammer is ___ useful tool.
7 '___ apple ___ day keeps the doctor away.'

▷ *the* is left out before plural nouns and mass nouns in general statements:
eg *Dogs make good pets; Sugar is bad for you;*
and in many fixed expressions:
eg *take place, by train, at school.*

**2** Fill in the blanks with a suitable determiner if needed:

> Chinese food is **the** best food in **the** world.

1 Which ___ animals make ___ best pets, ___ cats or ___ dogs?
2 How do you like ___ your coffee?
3 With ___ cream and ___ brown sugar.
4 Is ___ bullfighting ___ most popular sport in ___ Spain?
5 It is popular, especially with ___ tourists, but ___ sport that ___ most Spaniards enjoy is ___ football.
6 On ___ Saturdays, we usually have ___ dinner early and then go to ___ cinema.
7 ___ my wife and I go to ___ church on ___ Sunday morning, except when ___ children are on ___ holiday.
8 Do you go to ___ school on ___ foot?

Determiners I  2–4

9 No, we usually go on ____ bus.

10 'How do you start this car?'

'Put ____ key in ____ ignition, and turn it. Put ____ your foot on ____ accelerator, and, as long as there is ____ petrol in ____ tank, it should start.'

**3** Put in *a/an* or *the* where necessary:

> I'm very thirsty. May I have **a** glass of ____ water?

1 This is ____ picture of ____ house where I lived when I was ____ child.

2 ____ French people shake ____ hands more often than ____ English do.

3 Let me give you ____ piece of ____ advice.

4 Do you know ____ difference between ____ Great Britain and ____ United Kingdom?

5 I know that ____ Britain is not ____ same thing as ____ British Isles.

6 ____ trouble with ____ old furniture is that it is too big for ____ modern houses.

7 ____ Earth goes round ____ Sun.

8 'Have you got ____ library in your school?' 'Yes, and ____ teacher in ____ charge of it says that most of ____ books are out of ____ date.'

9 '____ best things in ____ life are free.'

▷ Remember: many fixed expressions miss out the article, eg *shake hands*.

**4** Put these nouns into the sentences:

Nouns: attention, breakfast, care, cold, friends, fun, jobs, place, time.

> What time do you usually have **breakfast**?

1 What time does the meeting take _____

2 We soon made _____ with our neighbours.

3 I know I'm silly, but please don't make _____ of me.

4 Will you take _____ of my dog while I'm away?

5 Put a warm coat on, or you might catch _____

7

## 4–5 Determiners I

**6** Please pay _____ to what I have to say.

**7** I hope we'll have _____ to visit you when we are in Zurich.

**8** I don't like working here: I'm thinking of changing _____

**5** Put the articles back into this story:

> What is meaning of word 'nice'?
> *What is the meaning of the word 'nice'?*

John is very good friend of mine. He is bus driver and his wife is waitress. They live in small house in centre of village. House has two bedrooms and small garden at back. They have two children, younger is boy, older is girl. Because house is so small, children have to share bedroom, but this is not problem because they are still very young. They go to same school. Because it is not far from house where they live, they usually go to school on foot except when weather is very bad. Then they take bus.

# Determiners 1   6

▷ Use *this*, plural *these*, for things near you in space or time.
Use *that*, plural *those*, for things not near you in space or time.

**6** Write sentences to fit these pictures:

__This__ is a hammer, and __those__ are nails.

**1** *(screwdriver/spanner)*

_____ is a screwdriver, and _____ is a spanner.

**2** *(screws/nuts and bolts)*

_____ are screws, and _____ are nuts and bolts.

**3** *(cat/mice)*

_____ is a cat, and _____ are mice.

**4** *(cakes/loaf of bread)*

_____ are cakes, and _____ is a loaf of bread.

**5** *(typewriter/computer)*

_____ is a typewriter, and _____ is a computer.

# 3 Determiners II
some / any / a lot of / plenty of; much / many / a little / a few / no / none

▷ These are words which describe quantity. *some* is used in statements and 'inviting' questions like *'Do you want some more tea?'*
*any* is used in negatives and in real questions, eg *I don't want any; Do you have any money on you?*
The same is true for compounds like *something, anybody,* etc.
*no* means the same as *not . . . any,* eg *I have no money = I haven't any money.*
Use *none* and compounds in short answers, eg *What are you doing? Nothing.*

**1** Fill in the blanks with a suitable determiner:

> I want **some** bread, but I don't need **any** cakes.

1  There's _____ brown bread left but we haven't got _____ more white.
2  Have you got _____ luggage with you?
3  Can't you do _____ thing right?
4  Would you like _____ more tea, Vicar?
5  She never seems to have _____ money.
6  'Who were you talking to?' '_____body!'
7  Did you tell _____ one that you were coming here today?
8  See if you can clear the table without dropping _____ thing!
9  'How many exercises have you done?' '_____ at all.'
10  _____ body's been sitting in my chair!

▷ *much* and *many* are used with *how, so, as* and *too. much* and *a little* are used with singular mass nouns, *many* and *a few* with plural count nouns.

**2** Fill in the blanks with a suitable determiner:

> 'Did you meet **any** interesting people at the party?' 'Only **a few.**'

1  'You haven't got _____ furniture, have you?' 'No, only a _____ pieces.'
2  Does a haircut cost as _____ as a shave?
3  'Have I put too _____ salt in this?' 'No, it needs a _____ more.'
4  I've spilled _____ drops of coffee on the carpet.

Determiners II 2–3

5 Well, there isn't _____ I can do about it, is there?
6 This will be a short letter, Mother, as I haven't got _____ news.
7 'How _____ money have you got?' 'Not _____.'
8 Eat as _____ fruit as you like.
9 Please try not to make so _____ mistakes in future!
10 A _____ knowledge is a dangerous thing.

3   Say what you can see in this picture:

I can see some motorbikes but I can't see any bicycles.
or There are some motorbikes but there aren't any bicycles.

1 _____ schoolgirls _____ schoolboys.
2 _____ dogs _____ cats.
3 _____ cars _____ buses.
4 _____ shops _____ churches.

## 4 Determiners II

**4** Rewrite these sentences so that they mean the same, using the words in brackets:

> How much money is there in the till? Just a little. (*dollars*)
> *There are a few dollars in the till.*

1 We've still got a little time to spare. (*minutes*)

2 I need some paper. Have you got any? (*notebook*)

3 Here are a few facts about Indonesia. (*information*)

4 'How much time did you spend in Florence?' 'Not much.' (*days*)

5 Could you put a few more logs on the fire? (*coal*)

6 We have a little orange juice, but not much milk. (*bottles of orange juice; cartons of milk*)

7 I need some cigarettes. Will you get me some? (*tobacco*)

8 Were there many cars in town? (*traffic*)

9 These are my suitcases. Where shall I put them? (*luggage*)

# 4 Determiners III
**all / every / each; both / either / neither**

▷ These words describe how things are distributed.
*all* and *both* join; *each*, *every*, *either* and *neither* separate.

**1** Rewrite these sentences choosing one of the words in brackets:

> I laugh (*every* / *all* / *either*) time I think of it.
> *I laugh every time I think of it.*

1 Here are two things. Do you want (*all* / *both* / *each*) of them?

Actually, I don't want (*either* / *neither* / *all*) of them.

2 Here are several things. Do you want (*both* / *all* / *every*) of them?

Actually, I don't want (*any* / *none* / *each*) of them.

3 Let's (*all* / *every* / *each*) go for a walk.

4 There were four cakes left, and I ate (*every one* / *everyone* / *every*) of them.

5 Father gave (*all* / *every* / *either*) the children a kiss, and gave (*both* / *all* / *each one*) a present.

6 'How much are the oranges?' '20 pence (*every* / *each* / *all*).'

7 I asked (*each* / *every* / *all*) my teachers the same question, and they (*both* / *each* / *every one*) gave me a different answer.

8 He had two choices, but he didn't want (*both* / *each* / *either*) of them.

## 1–2 Determiners III

9 Tell them (*all / everyone / each one*) that tomorrow is a holiday.
___

10 'Which colour do you prefer, the light blue or the dark blue?' 'I don't really like (*either / none / both*) of them.'
___

▷ *both* refers to two; *all* refers to more than two.

There are two patterns with pronouns, eg $\begin{array}{c}all\\both\end{array}$ of $\begin{array}{c}us\\them\\etc\end{array}$ and $\begin{array}{c}we\ all\\us\ both\\etc\end{array}$

**2** Replace the words underlined with a sentence for each of these patterns:

> He gave <u>me and my sisters</u> a present.
> *He gave all of us a present.*
> and
> *He gave us all a present.*

1 She told John and his brother to get out.
___
___

2 My wife and I like windsurfing.
___
___

3 Our three children prefer sailing.
___
___

4 The whole group would like to go.
___
___

5 They invited me and my family to stay for dinner.
___
___

# Determiners III   3

 *so* and *neither* are used to express agreement.

**3** Agree with these statements:

> 'I can swim.'
> '*So can I.*'
> 'I don't like tennis.'
> '*Neither do I.*'

1  I've got a headache.
   _____

2  I cannot pronounce this word.
   _____

3  I don't want to go home yet.
   _____

4  I'd like to be taller.
   _____

5  I wish I had long blond hair.
   _____

6  I'm going on holiday tomorrow.
   _____

7  I'll never forget this day!
   _____

8  I didn't understand a word she said.
   _____

# 5 Adjectivals

▷ Adjectivals are used to identify, eg *Which car? The red one, the car in the garage, the car I bought last week.*

1. There are several women in this picture, some tall, some short, some with children, some carrying shopping baskets. Identify each one:

I am looking at one of the short women. The one I am looking at is carrying a basket, but hasn't got a child.

1 _____

2 _____

3 _____

## Adjectivals 2–3

**2** Identify the different men in this picture, using adjectivals like:
*fat, thin*, and descriptions: *wearing a hat, standing next to a car/lamp post.*

1 _____

2 _____

3 _____

4 _____

▷ Word order of determiners and adjectivals before a noun phrase is fixed:
eg *some/all*, etc + *the/this/my*, etc + *first/next*, etc + *one, two, three*, etc + adjectives.

**3** Rewrite these sentences putting the words in brackets in the right order:

Would you like (*unused/last/three/the*) copies of the book?
*Would you like the last three unused copies of the book?*

1 These are (*school/my/all/old*) photographs.
_____

2 Nearly (*all/German/other/our*) friends live in Cologne.
_____

3 They say that (*last/six/all of/indoor/the*) meetings were cancelled.
_____

## 3–4 Adjectivals

4 I shall miss (*television / most of / five / next / her*) shows.

_____

5 It looks as if (*other / half of / these / green*) peppers are rotten.

_____

▷ Word order of adjectives is also usually fixed in this way:
quality / size / age / shape / colour / origin / material.

Reorder these phrases in a similar way:

> a (*wooden / small / round*) table
> a small round wooden table.

6 a (*grey-haired / little / French / pretty*) lady

_____

7 two (*landscape / famous / old*) paintings

_____

8 this (*Victorian / interesting / oval-shaped*) mirror

_____

9 a (*beautiful / young / Arab*) racehorse.

_____

10 a (*big / black and white / great*) sheepdog

_____

▷ Comparison of adjectives: most short adjectives add *-(e)r* and *-(e)st* (sometimes with spelling changes, eg *big bigger biggest*). In other cases, use *more* and *most*. There are a few irregular forms, eg *good better best*.

**4** Fill in the table below:

> | slow | slower | slowest |

1 big _____ _____   2 easy _____ _____

Adjectivals 4–5

3 sad _____ _____     10 fat _____ _____
4 early _____ _____   11 quiet _____ _____
5 flat _____ _____    12 far _____ _____
6 heavy _____ _____   13 narrow _____ _____
7 clean _____ _____   14 thin _____ _____
8 grey _____ _____    15 sunny _____ _____
9 common _____ _____  16 ill/bad _____ _____

**5** Rewrite these sentences using the appropriate comparative:

> = more adj/adj-er than, eg older than          = = as adj as, eg as old as
< = less adj than, eg less beautiful than         ≠ = not as/so adj as, eg not as beautiful as

---

Mount Everest        (high)        Mont Blanc.
                     >
_Mount Everest is higher than Mont Blanc._

---

1 Air              (light)        water.
                   >

_____

2 I find maths     (difficult)    physics.
                   <

_____

3 Water            (light)        air.
                   ≠

_____

4 A metre          (long)         a yard.
                   >

_____

## 5–6 Adjectivals

**5** Stealing   (bad)   telling lies.
   >

**6** Pluto   (distant)   Mars.
   >

**7** My father   (old)   my mother.
   ≠

**8** Fish   (common)   whales.
   >

**6** Use the words in brackets to make sentences in this pattern:

> That's a pretty dress! (*nice/see*)
> *That's the prettiest dress I have ever seen!*

1 This is a lovely steak. (*tasty/eat*)

2 What a marvellous car! (*fast/drive*)

3 He's a very intelligent man. (*clever/speak to*)

4 This is terrible beer. (*bad/drink*)

5 She doesn't say much. (*quiet/meet*)

# Adjectivals 7–8

▷ There are a number of useful expressions with the pattern: verb + adj, eg, *feel ill*.

**7** Choose one verb and one adjective from these lists for each sentence:

Verbs: come, ~~fall~~, feel, get, go, grow, keep, make, sit, turn
Adjectives: asleep, better, blue, ~~ill~~, mad, old, quiet, sure, still, true

> Jane was **feeling ill** so she went to the doctor's.

1 I was so tired that I _____ in the chair.

2 Do dreams ever _____

3 I hear you've been ill. I hope you _____ soon.

4 I think I'll _____ if I hear that song again!

5 My hair's grey and my teeth are falling out. I must be _____

6 Please _____ or you'll wake the baby.

7 Don't move! Just _____ while I cut your hair.

8 Have you put all the lights out?

   I'll just go and _____

9 He was so cold that his nose _____

▷ Nationalities: sometimes the word for the person is different from the nationality:

eg *I am from Spain, I am a Spaniard, my nationality is Spanish.*
Sometimes it is the same,
eg *I am from Norway, I am a Norwegian, my nationality is Norwegian.*

**8** Complete the table:

| I am from | I am a(n) | My nationality is |
|---|---|---|
| Norway | **Norwegian** | **Norwegian** |
| 1 Canada | _____ | _____ |
| 2 Spain | _____ | _____ |
| 3 Russia | _____ | _____ |
| 4 Germany | _____ | _____ |

## 8–9 Adjectivals

5 Turkey _____ _____
6 Finland _____ _____
7 Greece _____ _____
8 USA _____ _____
9 Poland _____ _____
10 Denmark _____ _____
11 Sweden _____ _____
12 Italy _____ _____
13 Scotland _____ _____
14 Portugal _____ _____
15 Switzerland _____ _____
16 Peru _____ _____
17 Japan _____ _____
18 Brazil _____ _____
19 Thailand _____ _____
20 Israel _____ _____

**9** Numbers: what are these numbers in words?

> 64
> _sixty-four_

1 79
_____

2 365
_____

3 1,542
_____

4 4,050
_____

5  14,500

6  100,000

7  203,654

8  1,330,000

9  0.75

10  3.76

How would you say these telephone numbers?

| 01 340 9355 | *oh one three four oh nine three double five* |

11  01-370-2299

12  052-600-2700

What are these dates in words?

| 19 October 2010 | *the nineteenth of October, two thousand and ten* |

13  12 April, 1989

14  August 14th, 1992

15  23rd May, 1066

# 6 Pronouns

▷ Pronouns refer to people or things, and stand instead of a noun phrase, eg *Bill loves Susan: he telephones her every day. This machine switches itself off.* Pronoun forms include the subject (eg *he*), object (eg *him*), possessive (eg *his*) and reflexive (eg *himself*).

**1** Complete the table:

| Singular | | | | | Plural | | | | |
|---|---|---|---|---|---|---|---|---|---|
| I | ____ | my | ____ | myself | ____ | ____ | ____ | ours | ourselves |
| you | you | your | ____ | ____ | you | you | your | ____ | ____ |
| he | ____ | his | his | ____ | | | | | |
| she | ____ | ____ | hers | herself | ____ | ____ | their | theirs | ____ |
| it | it | ____ | ____ | itself | | | | | |

**2** Fill in the blanks with the correct pronoun:

Anna always locks _her_ car when _she_ leaves _it_ in the street.

1 My father always washes _____ shirts _____ self.
2 Elizabeth has two children, and _____ loves _____ both.
3 If I tell you a secret, promise to keep _____ to _____ self.
4 People often forget to take _____ umbrellas with _____.
5 John and Mary hurt _____ selves playing squash.
6 We went on a picnic and Joe came with _____ . We all enjoyed _____ very much.
7 'Did your father make that boat for _____?' 'No, I made _____ all by _____.'
8 Some of these books belong to my brother and some to my sister, but I don't know which are _____ and which are _____.

# Pronouns 3

▷ The pronoun *it* is used in many impersonal expressions, eg *It's time to leave.*

**3** Write expressions to fit these pictures:

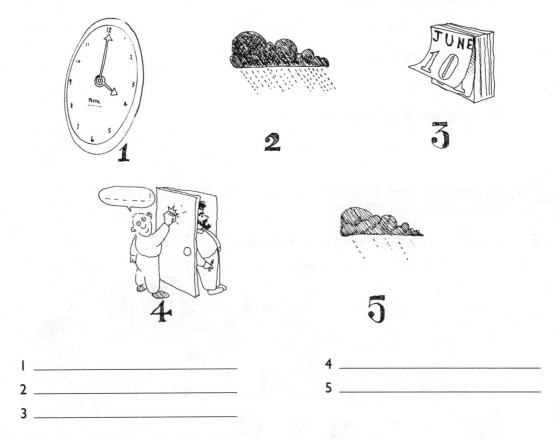

1 _____     4 _____
2 _____     5 _____
3 _____

Now write sentences from these prompts:

> drive carefully in town/important
> *It's important to drive carefully in town.*

**6** understand what he says/difficult

_____

**7** bring up a child on your own/hard

_____

**8** learn without a teacher/not easy

_____

## 3–4 Pronouns

9 know foreign languages/useful
_____

10 see yourself on video/funny
_____

11 say goodnight/a pity
_____

12 crying over spilt milk/no use
_____

▷ The word *there* is used in a similar way, eg, *There's a horse in the garden. There are some cows on the lawn.*

**4** Look at the picture and write eight sentences:

1 _____
2 _____
3 _____
4 _____
5 _____
6 _____
7 _____
8 _____

## Pronouns 5

**5** Choose the correct word. Only one is correct.

> 'Will you wash my car?' 'No, I won't! Wash
> - it yourself' ☑
> - it you' ☐
> - you it' ☐

1 Come and meet an old friend of
- me. ☐
- my. ☐
- mine. ☐

2 I have
- my ☐
- an ☐
- the ☐
own car now; I paid for it
- myself. ☐
- my own. ☐
- by me. ☐

3 There are two pears: give me
- an ☐
- one ☐
- it ☐
and keep
- another ☐
- the other ☐
- other one ☐
for
- you. ☐
- yours. ☐
- yourself. ☐

4 Your room is much tidier than
- my. ☐
- the my. ☐
- mine. ☐

5 Why do dogs always smell
- one another? ☐
- each the other? ☐
- themselves? ☐

6 Did you see the accident? Please describe
- it to me. ☐
- it me. ☐
- me it. ☐

7
- She ☐
- Her ☐
- To her ☐
was given a present.

8 Some people like brown sugar,
- others ☐
- another ☐
- the other ☐
prefer
- a white one. ☐
- white. ☐
- white one. ☐

9 John can't play because he's broken
- the ☐
- his ☐
- himself ☐
arm.

# 7 Prepositions

▷ Prepositions describe relationships, such as: space, eg *He's <u>in</u> the garden*; time, eg *I'll see you <u>after</u> the lesson*; method, eg *I opened the window <u>with</u> a knife*.

**1** Write sentences from the picture using these prepositions and nouns:
Prepositions: <u>across</u>, along, down, into, over, <u>past</u>, <u>round</u>, through, under, up
Nouns: bank, bridge, <u>church</u>, <u>corner</u>, gate, hill, park, river, <u>road</u>, steps

John walked across the road, past the church, round the corner....

# Prepositions 2

**2**

*This is the time now.*
*It was 8 o'clock when I last saw him.*

**Choose the correct time preposition from the list below:**
at, since, by, for, before, after, past

| I didn't see him **after** 8 o'clock. |
|---|

1  I last saw him _____ 8 o'clock.

2  I haven't seen him _____ 8 o'clock.

3  I haven't seen him _____ four hours.

*This is when I shall see him again.*

4  I'll see him again _____ 4 o'clock.

5  I shall not see him again _____ 4 o'clock.

*This is when I shall finish work.*

6  I shall work _____ 5 o'clock.

7  I shall have finished _____ 5 o'clock at the latest.

8  I shall not work _____ 5 o'clock.

## 3–4 Prepositions

▷ Adjectives may be followed by a preposition, eg *afraid of the dark*.

**3** Fill in the correct preposition:

> I am terrified **of** spiders.

1 Fresh fruit is good _____ you.
2 You ought to be ashamed _____ yourself!
3 He's not very good _____ foreign languages.
4 Are you very interested _____ sport?
5 I like football, but I'm not very keen _____ tennis.
6 Our son has passed his driving test: we are very proud _____ him.
7 This essay isn't very good: I'm still not satisfied _____ it.
8 He's not used _____ taking orders from a woman.
9 'Does he love her?' 'He's crazy _____ her!'
10 John's been absent _____ work since Monday.

**4** Many verbs are followed by a preposition, eg, *Look at this.*

Fill in one verb and one preposition in each sentence:

Verbs: thank, look, look, long, apologise, ~~pay~~, believe, congratulate, depend, lend, borrow, prevent, suffer, take.
Prepositions: after, after, ~~for~~, for, for, for, from, from, from, in, on, on, to.

> Who **paid** **for** the meal? I did.

1 I've _____ everywhere _____ my key, but I can't find it anywhere.
2 Will you _____ _____ the children while I go to the shops, please?
3 I'm fed up with work. I'm _____ _____ the summer holidays to arrive.
4 'I must _____ _____ being so late.' 'That's all right.'
5 You can't _____ _____ John: he'll always let you down.
6 Do you really _____ _____ ghosts?
7 _____ you _____ being such a good friend to me.
8 He _____ her _____ her success.

9 I never _____ money _____ relatives, or _____ money _____ friends.

10 He tied his horse to a tree to _____ it _____ getting away.

11 Do you _____ _____ hay fever in the summer?

12 Sarah _____ _____ her mother: she even dresses like her.

There are many fixed expressions having the pattern preposition + noun, eg *at school, in time*.

**5** Choose the right preposition to go with the noun in brackets and rewrite the sentence:

> Do it immediately. (*once*)
> *Do it at once.*

1 'Was it an accident?' 'No, he did it deliberately.' (*purpose*)

2 Learn this poem so that you can remember it. (*heart*)

3 This machine is not working. (*order*)

4 He is in his house. (*home*)

5 Please be a good boy because it will make me happy. (*sake*)

6 I know your boss because I have seen him, but I don't know his name. (*sight*)

7 I am leaving this town and I will never come back. (*good*)

8 He tried to persuade her to stay but he was not successful. (*vain*)

9 Please try to be punctual for the meeting. (*time*)

## 5–6 Prepositions

Some prepositions are compound, eg *with regard to*.

**6** Choose one word from each list to make the compound preposition you need:
List 1: according, apart, ~~because~~, except, in spite, instead
List 2: ~~of~~, of, for, from, of, to

> He had to give up his job **because of** ill health.

1 _____ _____ the weather forecast, it's going to snow soon.

2 We decided to go ahead with our picnic _____ _____ the rain.

3 Everyone had a good time, _____ _____ Stephanie, who left early.

4 Why don't you do something useful, _____ _____ just watching TV?

5 Everyone passed the exams _____ _____ John, who failed everything.

# 8 Introduction to verbs

▷ Regular verbs form the past participle in -(e)d, eg *I walk, I walked, I have walked*. There are about 100 common verbs which form the past and past participle in other ways, eg *see – saw – seen*.

**1** Complete the table:

| see | _saw_ | _seen_ |
|---|---|---|

1  choose  _____  _____
2  _____  felt  _____
3  put  _____  _____
4  _____  _____  paid
5  _____  _____  grown
6  call  _____  _____
7  _____  gave  _____
8  seem  _____  _____
9  _____  _____  lost
10  sell  _____  _____

11  _____  _____  beaten
12  _____  told  _____
13  catch  _____  _____
14  _____  became  _____
15  keep  _____  _____
16  _____  _____  fallen
17  cost  _____  _____
18  _____  ate  _____
19  _____  _____  driven
20  _____  showed  _____

**2** Say which of these irregular verbs has a different pattern from the other four, and write out the pattern:

| cut, see, hit, shut  _see_ | see  saw  seen |
|---|---|

The pattern of the others is the same: *cut cut cut, hit hit hit, shut shut shut.*

1  drink, think, swim, sing, begin  _____  _____
2  fight, think, bring, buy, teach  _____  _____
3  break, speak, steal, wear, wake  _____  _____
4  stand, lend, build, spend, bend  _____  _____
5  burst, let, set, hurt, shoot  _____  _____
6  throw, say, know, fly, blow  _____  _____

## 3–4 Introduction to verbs

**3** Write these sentences in the past simple:

> What did he do?
> (bite/his lip)     He bit his lip.

1 (draw/a picture)
2 (find/a mistake)
3 (forget/his key)
4 (light/a cigarette)
5 (make/a mistake)
6 (send/her a letter)
7 (tear/his shirt on a nail)
8 (write/a very good essay)

**4** Write these sentences in the present perfect:

> What have you done?
> (bite/lip)     I've bitten my lip.

1 (draw/picture)
2 (find/mistake)
3 (forget/my key)
4 (light/a cigarette)
5 (make/mistake)
6 (send/letter to her)
7 (tear/my shirt on a nail)
8 (write/an essay)

Introduction to verbs 5–6

**5** Choose the right tense of the verb in these sentences:

> It was so cold that the River Thames _froze_ over. (freeze)

1 John hasn't _____ home yet. (come)
2 Where have you _____ the Christmas presents? (hide)
3 'Has Janet _____ yet?' 'Yes, she _____ an hour ago.' (leave, leave)
4 I _____ to London and I _____ the Queen. (go, meet)
5 This door is _____. (stick)
6 The meeting was _____ in the Church Hall. (hold)
7 She still hasn't _____ him for getting drunk. (forgive)
8 I _____ to go out last night, but I just _____ reading instead. (mean, sit)
9 We have _____ out of food. (run)
10 There were no rooms free, so I _____ at the railway station. (sleep)

▷ The simple tenses (*I see, I saw*), form questions and negatives with a part of the verb *do*, eg *Do you see? Did they see? She doesn't see. We didn't see.* Other tenses do not, eg, *He has left, Has he left? He hasn't left.*

**6** Make questions with the words in brackets (be careful with the tense):

> I like potatoes. (*you?*)
> _Do you like potatoes?_

1 I got a letter this morning. (*she?*)
_____

2 He studies physics. (*you?*)
_____

3 I heard a strange noise. (*you?*)
_____

4 My students are very clever. (*your students?*)
_____

## 6–8 Introduction to verbs

**5** We have read a lot of Dickens. (*the others?*)
_____

**6** She'll be away for a week. (*her brother?*)
_____

**7** Someone rang the doorbell. (*you?*)
_____

**8** I want some more tea. (*you?*)
_____

▷ Modals and parts of *do*, *be* and *have* form short forms with *not*, eg *can't, don't, aren't, hadn't*. Many of them also have short forms with pronouns, eg *I'm, we'll, he'd*.

**7** Make negatives of these verbs to complete the sentence:

> I like potatoes, but _I don't like_ meat.

1 We went out on Monday, but _____ on Thursday.
2 He can play football, but _____ tennis.
3 I did the first test, but _____ the second one.
4 I won a small prize, but _____ any money.
5 I'll cut the lawn, but _____ the hedge.
6 He shook his head, but _____ my hand.
7 I've got a brother, but _____ any sisters.
8 He speaks Spanish, but _____ Catalan.

**8** Add question tags to these statements:

> He's a doctor, _isn't he?_

1 You went out last night, _____
2 They're Polish, _____
3 We must be careful, _____

Introduction to verbs 8–9

4 We'll be all right, _____

5 You can swim, _____

6 You'd always tell me the truth, _____

7 Let's go, _____

8 John's still at work, _____

9 John's gone to America, _____

10 We've got tomorrow off, _____

**9** Write short answers to these questions:

| Does Jane live here? | No, she **doesn't**. |

1 Can you speak Russian?   No, I _____
2 Have they arrived yet?   No, they _____
3 Have you any money left?   No, we _____
4 Could you help us?   No, I _____
5 Were the boys at the party?   No, they _____
6 Will John pay for the meal?   No, he _____
7 Did anyone call while I was out?   No, they _____
8 Are you sure about that?   No, I _____

# 9 Simple and continuous forms

▷ The present simple tells you what usually happens; the present continuous tells you what is happening at the time of speaking.

1  Say what the different people in the picture are doing:

People: postman, policeman, doctor, sailor, roadsweeper

Actions: hold a broom, look through a telescope, ride a bicycle, stand on one's hands, wear shoes.

Other words: backwards, the wrong end, upside down

| The postman _is riding a bicycle backwards._ |

1 _____
2 _____
3 _____
4 _____

Say what the people in the picture usually do. The following words will help you:
Actions: go to sea, deliver, direct, keep clean, look after.

| Postmen _usually deliver letters._ |

5 Policemen _____
6 Doctors _____
7 Sailors _____
8 Roadsweepers _____

## Simple and continuous forms 2

**2** Write questions to fit the answers, using the words in brackets:

> (get up) **When/What time do you get up?**
> Usually about eight thirty.

1 (get paid) _____

   Every Friday.

2 (this evening) _____

   I'm going out with my parents.

3 (leave school) _____

   When I was seventeen.

4 (shopping) _____

   About twice a week.

5 (last night) _____

   I stayed in.

6 (go / when I saw you) _____

   I was on my way to the doctor's.

7 (married) _____

   In 1987.

8 (your daughter) _____

   Studying medicine at London University.

9 (languages) _____

   French, Spanish and a little German.

10 (hurt) _____

   I fell off my bike.

## 3 Simple and continuous forms

▷ Words referring to states (measurement, possession, the senses) are usually in the present simple, eg *This line measures 12 cm*. If you are talking about an action, they can also be in the present continuous, eg *The tailor is measuring me for a new suit*.

**3** Look at the pictures and complete the sentences using simple and continuous forms:

(*measure*)
This line **measures 100 yards.**
The tailor **is measuring him** for a new suit.

(*weigh*)
1 The man _____ himself.
   The piece of meat _____

(*have*)
2 The Smiths _____.
   They _____

(*smell*)
3 The man _____ the wine.
   The wine _____

## Simple and continuous forms 3–4

(*hold*)
**4** This petrol can _____

The little girl _____

(*take*)
**5** Mother _____ to school.

This parking meter _____ 20p coins.

▷ Sometimes a verb has a different meaning when it is used in the continuous form.

**4**
**1 a** We had a lot of pets when we were young.
Does 'have' mean 'possess' here?    YES   NO
**b** We were having dinner when George and his family arrived.
Does 'have' mean 'possess' here?    YES   NO
**2 a** How much does your petrol tank hold?
Does 'hold' mean 'handle' here?    YES   NO
**b** How many cards do you think am I holding in my hand?
Does 'hold' mean 'handle' here?    YES   NO
**3 a** Joe is very silly.
Is Joe silly by nature?    YES   NO
**b** John is being very silly.
Is John silly by nature?    YES   NO
**4 a** I expect you are tired after your journey.
Does 'expect' mean 'wait for' here?    YES   NO
**b** I'm expecting a parcel.
Does 'expect' mean 'wait for' here?    YES   NO
**5 a** What do you think of this picture?
Does 'think' mean 'have an opinion' here?    YES   NO
**b** What are you thinking about?
Does 'think' mean 'have an opinion' here?    YES   NO

## 5  Simple and continuous forms

**5** Which form fits? Note: more than one form may fit, so tick all the correct forms.

1. The coach
   - will leave ☐
   - leaves ☐
   - is leaving ☐
   
   in five minutes' time.

2. I
   - used to be ☐
   - was being ☐
   - was once ☐
   
   a heavy smoker.

3. 
   - Did you come ☐
   - Do you come ☐
   - Are you coming ☐
   
   to the dance tonight?

4. Please
   - sit ☐
   - be sitting ☐
   - to sit ☐
   
   down.

5. I
   - have ☐
   - got ☐
   - have got ☐
   
   something to tell you.

6. 
   - I work ☐
   - I'll be working ☐
   - I'm working ☐
   
   until 10 o'clock this evening.

# 10 Perfect tenses

▷ The perfect tenses are formed with *have*, eg *John has finished. They had already left. It has been snowing.* They are used to describe an action which took place between the past and the time of speaking, eg *Why are you crying? Because I've lost my purse.*

**1** Say what has happened:

> You can see a child crying. What has happened?
> (*lose/purse*)  _She's lost her purse._

You can see:
1 a girl lying on the ground

   (*fall/bicycle*) _____

2 a man holding a pair of glasses with a cracked lens

   (*break/glasses*) _____

3 a shopping basket on the ground

   (*drop/shopping basket*) _____

4 a policeman with a torn trouser leg

   (*dog/bite*) _____

5 a broken shop window

   (*lorry/go through*) _____

6 a car with the wheels missing

   (*thief/steal*) _____

**2** You saw the street scene in 1 yesterday. Tell your friend what you saw and what had happened.

> There was a child **who had lost her purse.** (*purse*)

1 There was a girl _____ (*bicycle*)

2 There was a man _____ (*glasses*)

3 There was a man _____ (*basket*)

4 There was a policeman _____ (*trousers*)

5 There was a lorry _____ (*shop window*)

6 There was a thief _____ (*car wheels*)

## 3–4 Perfect tenses

▷ The present perfect continuous is often used when we can see the results of an action which was going on up to or just before the time of speaking, eg, *There are no cars on the road* (result) *because it's been snowing* (activity).

**3** Complete these sentences showing Activity and Result:

|  | Result | Activity |
|---|---|---|
|  | (no cars) | (it/snow) |

There are no cars because it's been snowing.

1 (The girl)      (tired)      (work too hard)

_____

2 (The little boy)      (coughing)      (smoke/father's cigars)

_____

3 (The boys)      (wet)      (swim/lake)

_____

4 (The man)      (angry)      (wait/ages)

_____

5 (The roads)      (wet)      (rain)

_____

**4** You saw the scenes in 3 yesterday. Tell your friend what you saw.

(There were no cars)

There were no cars because it had been snowing.

1 (The girl was tired)

_____

2 (The little boy was coughing)

_____

Perfect tenses 4–5

**3** *(The boys were wet)*

_____

**4** *(The man was angry)*

_____

**5** *(The roads were wet)*

_____

▷ The perfect tenses are used with adverbials that express a time between the past and the time of speaking, eg, *recently, in the last few months*. The past simple is used when there is an adverbial which specifies an exact time, eg *last week, when I was at school*.

**5** Complete these sentences putting the verb in the correct form for the time expressions:

| Action | Time expression |
|---|---|
| (not see her) | for ages |

I *haven't seen her for ages.*

**1** *(not go out at all)*      last week

_____

**2** *(not go out much)*      recently

_____

**3** *(do a lot of work)*      during the last few days

_____

**4** *(not play football)*      since I was at school

_____

**5** *(not able to do much work)*      lately

_____

**6** *(go swimming a lot)*      when I was at school

_____

# 11 The future

▷ There are several ways of expressing the future, depending on your attitude to the future event, eg. *He will leave right away. He is leaving soon, he leaves for America next week; I'm going to leave you now.*

1 Choose the right form of the verb in these dialogues, and tick the box. Only one form is correct.

1

A Why 
- don't □
- won't □ we go shopping tomorrow?
- shan't □

B But tomorrow
- will be □
- is □ Sunday.  All the shops
- is going to be □

- are going to close. □
- are closing. □
- will be closed. □

A OK,
- we are going □
- we go □ swimming instead.
- we'll go □

2

A
- Shall you come □
- Do you come □ to the filmshow with me tonight?
- Will you come □

B That's very kind of you. I'd love to.

A OK,
- I'm seeing □
- I'll see □ you later then.
- I see □

3

A
- Do you come □
- Will you be coming □ to the filmshow tonight?
- Are you to come □

B
- I'll come □
- I come □ if it
- I'm coming □

- doesn't finish □
- won't finish □ too late.
- isn't finishing □

46

*The future* 1–2

A Don't worry. It   is finished ☐
                    will finish ☐   by ten at the latest.
                    is finishing ☐

**4**

A I've got to take all this luggage upstairs.   Will you help ☐
                                                Are you helping ☐ me, please?
                                                Do you help ☐

B I'm sorry, I can't.   I'll take ☐
                        I'm taking ☐ an exam in five minutes' time.
                        I take ☐

**2**   Do the same for this exercise:

1

A Do you think it   is going to rain ☐
                    is raining ☐ this afternoon?
                    rains ☐

B Why? What   do you do ☐
              are you doing ☐ this afternoon?
              will you do ☐

A Well, if it   will be ☐            go ☐
                is being ☐ fine, I   shall go ☐ for a cycle ride.
                is ☐                 will have gone ☐

B What a good idea!   I'm coming ☐
                      I come ☐ with you!
                      I'll come ☐

2

A What happens when you   add ☐
                          are adding ☐ $SO_3$ to water?
                          will add ☐

B You   get ☐
        are getting ☐ sulphuric acid.
        will be getting ☐

47

## 2  The future

**A** And what happens if you
- are going to put ☐
- will put ☐
- put ☐

your right hand into the acid?

**B** You
- will have ☐
- must ☐
- are needing ☐

to change your name to 'Lefty'.

### 3

**A**
- I'm going to be ☐
- I'll be ☐
- I am ☐

with you as soon as
- I'll have finished. ☐
- I've finished. ☐
- I'm finishing. ☐

**B** There's no hurry. We
- aren't being ☐
- shan't be ☐
- cannot be ☐

able to leave until ten, anyway.

### 4

**A** Mother
- shall be ☐
- is going to be ☐
- is ☐

very angry when she
- sees ☐
- will see ☐
- is seeing ☐

what you have done.

**B** I bet she
- isn't even noticing! ☐
- isn't even going to notice! ☐
- won't even notice! ☐

# The future 3

▷ The expression *going to* is used to give warnings and to make predictions, eg *It's going to rain soon* (when you see black clouds in the sky).

**3** Make predictions from the picture using *going to*:

(rain)
It _is going to rain_ soon.

(fall off)
1 He _____ if he's not careful!

(cut)
2 She _____ if she doesn't watch out.

(run over)
3 You're _____ that dog if you're not careful.

(have an accident)
4 The taxi driver _____ if he's not careful.

(spill the wine)
5 The waiter _____ any second now!

(start fighting)
6 Those two men _____ in a minute!

## 4  The future

▷ The tense in time clauses after the future and after real condition *if* clauses, is always present or present perfect, eg *I'll join you when I'm ready* (not *will be ready*).

**4** Finish the sentences using the words in brackets:

> I'll join you when __I'm ready.__ (be ready)

1  We'll leave as soon as the film _____ (finish)

2  Stay here until I _____ (send for you)

3  We won't go unless he _____ (tell us to)

4  Let's take our anoraks in case it _____ (start to rain)

5  He'll come back once he _____ (run out of money)

6  Don't do it if you _____ (not want to)

7  We can watch TV after we _____ (have dinner)

8  I will do it if she _____ (ask me)

# 12 Modals

▷ The modals include *can/could + able to, may/might, must + have to, need* and *dare*. They express such ideas as possibility and probability.

**1** Fill in the blanks with *must,* or part of *have to*:

> Yesterday, I **had to** go and see my bank manager.

1 Tomorrow I _____ walk to school.
2 I don't mind _____ walk to school.
3 I _____ wear glasses ever since I was thirteen.
4 Try to get through this month without _____ borrow from your father.
5 I hope I _____ (not) _____ borrow money from him.
6 If you don't give me a lift, I _____ walk to work.
7 There's a hole in the roof: we're _____ pay a lot to get it repaired.
8 You're fat: you really _____ try to lose some weight.
9 'I have to wait six months for my new car.'
   He told me that he _____ wait six months for his new car.
10 'I had to wait six months for my new car.'
   He told me that he _____ wait six months for his new car.

▷ *was able to* is used instead of *could* (past) to suggest that you managed to do something or succeeded in doing something.

**2** Fill in the blanks with *can/could* or part of *able to*:

> The window was stuck, so I **couldn't** open it.

1 I'm sorry I _____ see you last night: I had to work late.
2 I'm sorry I _____ see you tonight: I have to work late.
3 If I'd had more time, I _____ come with you.
4 '_____ (you) _____ get in touch with John yet?'
   'No, I'll try again later.'

## 2–3 Modals

**5** You _____ believe anything he says: he is a terrible liar.

**6** I wonder if you _____ tell me the way to Guildford, please?

**7** I'm afraid I shall not _____ help you.

**8** To be a pilot, you need to _____ react quickly.

**9** Why haven't you posted those letters? You _____ done it when you were in town.

**10** I'd forgotten his telephone number so I _____ phone him.

**3** Choose the correct form of the modal *have to / be able to*:

> I might (*can*) sell my car.
> *I might be able to sell my car.*

**1** You may (*must*) pump the tyres up before you ride that bicycle.
_____

**2** To be an engineer, you must (*can*) do mathematics.
_____

**3** You should (*can*) to do this exercise if you try.
_____

**4** If she can't do it by herself, I may (*must*) help her.
_____

**5** If you hurry, you ought (*can*) catch the six-thirty.
_____

**6** When I was at school, we (*must*) be able to do arithmetic in our heads.
_____

**7** If you miss the last bus, you might (*must*) walk home.
_____

**8** If you had missed the last bus, you might (*must*) walk home.
_____

# Modals 4–5

**4** Fill in the blanks with *can't be, could be, may be, might be* or *must be*.
In some cases, more than one may fit.

What on earth is that?

It **must be** a camel, because it has a hump.

1 No, it _____ a camel, because camels don't have such long necks.
2 Well, it _____ a giraffe, then, because it's got a long neck.
3 No, it _____ a giraffe, because giraffes don't have humps.
4 OK, then. Do you think it _____ a lion?
5 No, it _____ a lion, because lions have sharp teeth!
6 I think it _____ an elephant.
   Why?
7 Well, it _____ an elephant. Look at its feet!
8 No, it _____ an elephant. It hasn't got a trunk.
9 In that case, there's only one thing it _____ : it's an giraffelephacamelion.
10 You _____ joking! There's no such animal!

**5** Study these pairs of sentences and then circle the right answer:

1 a You must be in bed by nine o'clock at the latest!
   This is                              **AN ORDER    A PIECE OF ADVICE**
  b You ought to be in bed by nine o'clock at the latest.
   This is                              **AN ORDER    A PIECE OF ADVICE**

# 5  Modals

**2 a** You mustn't do exercises 3 and 4.
   'mustn't' means   **NOT OBLIGED TO   OBLIGED NOT TO**
  **b** You don't have to do exercises 3 and 4.
   'mustn't' means   **NOT OBLIGED TO   OBLIGED NOT TO**

**3 a** I say: 'It's twelve o'clock'.
   I am   **STATING A FACT   MAKING A GUESS**
  **b** I say: 'It must be twelve o'clock'.
   I am   **STATING A FACT   MAKING A GUESS**

**4 a** They should be here by ten o'clock.
   At what time was this said?   **BEFORE 10   AFTER 10**
  **b** They should have been here by ten o'clock.
   At what time was this said?   **BEFORE 10   AFTER 10**

**5 a** I had plenty of time to catch my train, so I needn't have hurried.
   Did I in fact hurry?   **YES   NO   DON'T KNOW**
  **b** I had plenty of time to catch my train, so I didn't need to hurry.
   Did I in fact hurry?   **YES   NO   DON'T KNOW**

**6 a** You needn't speak so loudly.
   What does this express?   **AN ORDER   A PIECE OF ADVICE**
  **b** You mustn't speak so loudly.
   What does this express?   **AN ORDER   A PIECE OF ADVICE**

**7 a** I shall see you tomorrow.
   What does this express?   **A PROBABILITY   A CERTAINTY**
  **b** I might see you tomorrow.
   What does this express?   **A PROBABILITY   A CERTAINTY**

# 13 Conditionals

Conditional statements may be about
(1) the real world, eg *If you touch me, I'll scream. If (= whenever) $SO_3$ is added to $H_2O$, the result is $H_2SO_4$.*
(2) the imaginary world, eg *If I were rich, I would ask the princess to marry me.*
(3) what might (not) have happened, eg *If I had worked harder at school, I would have gone to University.*
Modals can be used in conditional sentences, eg, *If I'd worked harder at school, I might have been able to go to University.*

**1** Write a conditional sentence from the words given:

| Condition | Result | |
|---|---|---|
| (sugar/petrol tank) | (engine/not start) | |

*If you put sugar in the petrol tank, the engine won't start.*

1 (lighted match/petrol) — (an explosion)

2 (play with knives) — (cut yourself)

3 (take these pills) — (feel better)

4 (ask me to dance) — (say 'Yes')

5 (lion's tail) — (eat you) — (use *might*)

6 (save your money) — (buy yourself a house) — (use *be able*)

7 (practise hard) — (concert pianist) — (use *could*)

8 (study hard) — (a degree) — (use *should*)

## 2 Conditionals

*Poor John!*

**2** Complete the sentences using a suitable conditional:

> Poor John! He is unhappy because he has no school leaving certificate.
> What if he had a school leaving certificate?
>
> He __would be__ much happier if he had a certificate.

1 If he had a certificate, he _____ job as a postman.

2 If he was a postman, he _____ £100 a week.

3 If _____ £100 a week, he _____ buy a house.

4 Once he _____ a house, he _____ married.

5 Once he was married, he and his wife _____ lots of children.

6 But as soon as he had a family, he _____ more money.

7 If he _____ money, he would _____ a better job.

8 He couldn't get a better job unless he _____ for a degree.

Conditionals 2–3

9 He could only get a degree if he _____ a student again.

10 If he _____ a student, he _____ no money.

11 What would happen then? His wife and children _____

12 And John? He _____ as unhappy as he is now!

**3** Study these sentences and then circle the right answer:

1 a If I have enough time, I'll take a holiday this autumn.
  Will there be enough time this autumn?               YES   NO   DON'T KNOW
  b If I had enough time, I'd take a holiday this autumn.
  Will there be enough time this autumn?               YES   NO   DON'T KNOW
2 a If you drop eggs, they break.
  Am I talking about any particular eggs?                    YES   NO
  b If you drop those eggs, they'll break.
  Am I talking about any particular eggs?                    YES   NO
3 a I'd go right away if I were you.
  Is it too late for you to go?                              YES   NO
  b I'd have gone right away if I'd been you.
  Is it too late for you to go?                              YES   NO
4 a We'll go to Cardiff if it rains.
  If we go to Cardiff, what will the weather be?            FINE   WET
  b We'll go to Cardiff unless it rains.
  If we go to Cardiff, what will the weather be?            FINE   WET
5 a If you'd made any more mistakes, you would have lost your job.
  Is he likely to lose his job now?                    YES   NO   DON'T KNOW
  b If you make any more mistakes, you will lose you job.
  Is he likely to lose his job now?                    YES   NO   DON'T KNOW

# 14 The passive

▷ The passive is used when we want to put the object of a verb first, eg
*We use the passive* becomes *The passive is used (by us)*. It is formed from
part of *be* + past participle, eg. *It is used, it was used, it is being used.*

**1** Fill in each blank with a passive form of a verb from the list
below:

Verbs: allow, award, build, ~~build~~, dedicate, give, keep, plant, reach, send in

> This house **was built** in 1888.

1 You _____ (not) _____ on the grass.

2 This book _____ to Jenny.

3 These houses _____ by MacAlpine.

4 Tomorrow's lecture _____ by Prof Heisenberg.

5 The target _____ (not yet) _____ .

6 This oak tree _____ in 1953.

7 A prize _____ for the best essay.

All essays should _____ by next Thursday.

8 All dogs must _____ on a lead.

▷ The indirect object of verbs like *give* and *tell* can also become the
subject of a passive sentence, eg *They gave John a prize* → *John was given a prize*.

**2** Change these sentences into the passive:

> John <u>received</u> a prize (*give*)
> **John was given a prize.**

1 I <u>saw</u> the Crown Jewels. (*show*)

2 We were <u>finding out</u> how to make TNT. (*show*)

3 You <u>will now hear</u> the truth. (*tell*)

*The passive* 2–3

**4** I want to hear the truth. (*tell*)
_____

**5** These students are learning the passive. (*teach*)
_____

**6** They have answered a lot of questions. (*ask*)
_____

**7** You might receive a food parcel soon. (*send*)
_____

**8** He cannot go out. (*allow*)
_____

**3**   What do these notices mean?

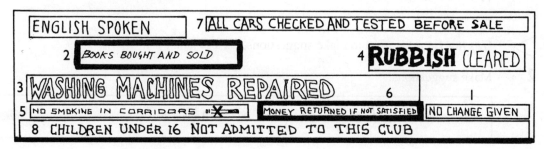

ENGLISH SPOKEN
Someone in this shop *speaks English.*

1 This machine _____
2 This is a shop where you _____
3 If your washing machine has broken down, we _____
4 We _____
5 You _____
6 If you are not satisfied, we _____
7 Before you buy a car from us, we _____
8 This club _____

# 15 The imperative

▷ The imperative is used to give warnings, instructions and orders, or to make requests and suggestions. The base form of the verb is used for the imperative, eg *Look out! Go! Listen!*

**1** Where would you expect to see these notices?

| NOTICE | PLACE |
|---|---|
| 1 KEEP TO THE RIGHT | a on the Underground |
| 2 KEEP OUT | b above a low doorway |
| 3 DON'T CROSS THE LINES | c on private property |
| 4 SWITCH OFF BEFORE LEAVING | d on a bottle of medicine |
| 5 MIND YOUR HEAD | e on a farm gate |
| 6 STORE IN A COOL, DRY PLACE | f on a deodorant stick |
| 7 RING BELL AND WAIT | g on the door of a surgery |
| 8 BEWARE OF BULL | h on a case containing a key |
| 9 MIND THE GAP | i at a railway station |
| 10 BREAK GLASS | j on an escalator |
| 11 PUSH UP BOTTOM | k in an office |

▷ *Let's* (for *Let us*) is used to make suggestions, *Let's go for a walk.*

**2** Make suggestions:

> It's a lovely day. **Let's go for a walk.** (walk)

1 It's raining. _____ (stay in/TV)

2 I'm starving. _____ (something to eat)

3 I'm tired out. Aren't you? _____ (bed)

4 There's a lot of filing to do. _____ (together)

5 I'm bored stiff. _____ (party)

*The imperative* 3

▷ *Let* is also used to mean *allow*, eg *Don't let him get away.* → *Don't allow him to get away.*

**3** Write sentences for the pictures:
Verbs: drink, drive, get away, go out, pick, play

 Don't let the baby drink the wine.

1 _____

2  _____

3  _____

4  _____

5   _____

## 4  The imperative

▷ Expressions like *Can/Could you . . . Will/Would you . . . please?* and *Do/Would you mind . . .?* are used to make an imperative more polite, eg *Tell me something* → *Could you tell me something, please?*

**4** Make these expressions more polite. (please!)

> Close the door. (could)
> *Could you close the door, please?*

1 Be quiet! (would)

2 Put your books away. (will)

3 Tell me what you're doing. (mind)

4 Help me with these suitcases. (could)

5 Don't do that! (mind)

6 Keep your dog under control. (would)

7 Leave me alone! (will)

8 Hurry up! (could)

9 Pass the salt. (mind)

10 Don't make so much noise. (mind)

# 16 Gerund and infinitive

▷ The gerund (formed by adding *-ing* to the base of the verb) is used as a noun, and after prepositions, eg *Swimming is good exercise. I'm bad at getting up in the morning.* Some verbs are followed by the gerund, others by the infinitive with or without *to*, eg *Avoid talking to strangers. I want to go home. Let me stay.*

**1** Choose the infinitive or gerund form to follow the verb in brackets:

> He _managed to pass_ his test. (*manage*)

1. He ___succeed to lose___ the weights. (*succeed*)
2. He/She _____ long letters. (*be used to*)
3. He/She _____ the car started. (*manage*)
4. He/She _____ dinner. (*refuse*)
5. He is no _____ jokes. (*good at*)
6. He _____ on holiday. (*think of*)
7. He _____ a good boy in future. (*promise*)
8. He/She _____ mistakes. (*keep*)
9. They have _____ nuclear weapons. (*agree*)
10. He should _____ so many potatoes. (*avoid*)

**2** Choose the infinitive or gerund form to go with the verb:

> I work in the garden.
> I enjoy _working in the garden._

1. I bite my fingernails.
   I can't help _____.
2. I do a lot of homework.
   I don't mind _____

## 2–3 Gerund and infinitive

**3** This essay must be finished by Friday.

I hope _____

**4** Did I lend you a fiver? (£5)

I don't remember _____

**5** I don't think I could swim a length underwater.

I've never tried _____

**6** I am surprised to see you here.

I didn't expect _____

**7** This letter doesn't need a reply.

I shall not bother _____

**8** I must be nice to my Aunt Maria.

I dislike _____

**9** I can look after myself.

I believe in _____

**10** I'd like a new car, but I haven't got enough money.

I cannot afford _____

**3** Choose the correct form of the verb:

**1** I want you    to try ☒   try ☐   trying ☐   harder.

**2** I'm looking forward   to see ☐   seeing ☒   to seeing ☒   you again.

**3** Please let me   go ☒   going ☒   to go ☐   by myself.

**4** I wish you would stop   drinking ☒   to drink ☐   drink ☐   so much.

Gerund and infinitive  3–4

5 Do you really expect
- that I believe ☐
- me believing ☐ you?
- me to believe ☒

6 It's much too late
- for going ☒
- to go ☒ out now.
- going ☐

7 It's no use
- you telling ☒
- that you tell ☐ me your troubles!
- you to tell ☒

8 Do you enjoy
- make ☐ people laughing? ☐
- to make ☐ people to laugh? ☒
- making ☒ people laugh? ☒

9 Do you mind
- me to close ☐
- if I close ☒ the window?
- for my closing ☐

10 I hope you didn't forget
- post ☐
- posting ☐ my letter.
- to post ☒

**4** Study these sentences and then circle the right answer:

1 a John has stopped to talk to Mary.
   Is he talking to her at this moment?  YES  NO

 b John has stopped talking to Mary.
   Is he talking to her at this moment?  YES  NO

2 a Do you remember putting this cake in the washing machine?
   Is there a cake in the washing machine?  YES  NO  DON'T KNOW

 b Did you remember to put the cake in the washing machine?
   Is there a cake in the washing machine?  YES  NO  DON'T KNOW

3 a 'I've got hiccups.'
   'Try holding your breath'.
   Does 'try' mean 'see if you can do it' here  YES  NO

 b 'How long can you hold your breath? Try to hold it for two minutes.'
   Does 'try' mean 'see if you can do it' here  YES  NO

# 17 Participles

▷ The participles are used in several common expressions, eg *go shopping, see someone doing something, get something done, something needs doing*; and to form adjectives, eg *an interesting book, a well-spoken woman*. The present participle is formed by adding *-ing* to the base form of the verb, eg *going*; the past participle by adding *-ed*, eg *dressed* (except for irregular verbs, eg *spoken*).

**1** Answer these questions by looking at the pictures:

| 1 dancing | 2 swimming | 3 windsurfing | 4 climbing |
| 5 skiing | 6 horseriding | 7 fishing | 8 bowling |

*shopping* — Where have you been? **I've been shopping.**

1 What are you doing this evening?

We are thinking of ___dancing___

2 What did you do last weekend?

We all _____

3 Have you got any plans for the weekend?

Yes, if it's windy, we _____

4 What'll you do if it's fine tomorrow?

_____

5 Where's Mary gone for her holidays?

_____ in Austria.

Participles 1–2

**6** What would you like to do today?

I wouldn't mind _____

**7** Where did your father take you yesterday?

He _____

**8** What would you have done if it had been raining?

We _____ instead.

▷ *It needs doing* really means *It needs to be done*.

**2** Write sentences from the pictures using the verbs below with *need*:

Verbs: ~~cut~~, cut, feed, iron (press), mend, repair, throw away, tidy up, wash

What needs doing?

The grass **needs cutting.**

1 The curtains _____

2 The man's trousers _____

3 The child's hair _____

## 2–3  Participles

4  The flowers _____

5  The whole room _____

6  The windows _____

7  The TV set _____

8  The dog will soon _____

▷ *get/have something done* is used when you will employ someone else to do a job for you, eg *I must get my hair cut.*

**3**  Choose one verb from the list to fit each of the sentences below:

alter, ~~cut~~, fix, mend, repair, see to, test

> Your hair looks terrible.
>
> I know, I must *get it cut.*

1  The car has broken down. What are you going to do about it?

   I _____

2  The TV set wouldn't work. Now it's OK. What did you do to it?

   Oh, I _____

3  The boiler sounds very noisy, doesn't it?

   Yes, I suppose _____

4  I've put on weight since I bought this dress.

   Well, you could always _____

5  You can't go to an interview with your hair in such a mess!

   I know, I'm _____

6  I can't read this.

   It's your eyes. You _____

# Participles 4

▷ Participles are also used as adjectives, eg *an interesting story, a well-spoken woman.*

**4** Make an adjective from each verb in the list to fit the sentences below:

bore, break, curve, disappoint, dress, excite, knit, lay, make, speak, terrify

> A woman with a very pleasant and educated voice is
> a **well-spoken woman.**

1 A man who wears very good clothes is

   a well-_____

2 An adventure that you enjoyed very much was

   an _____

3 A pullover that your mother made for you is

   a _____

4 An experience that really frightened you was

   a _____

5 A promise that you don't keep is

   a _____

6 Jam that is not bought in a shop is

   home-_____

7 A performance which did not please people was

   a _____

8 A line that looks like the letter C is

   a _____

9 An egg that is absolutely fresh is

   a new-_____

10 Children who cannot find anything to do are

   _____

## 4–5 Participles

**5** Study these sentences and then circle the right answer:

**1 a** I watched some men digging a hole in the road.
Did I watch until they had finished?      YES   NO   DON'T KNOW

**b** I watched some men dig a hole in the road.
Did I watch until they had finished?      YES   NO   DON'T KNOW

**2 a** I thought that Janet was very interesting in the play.
Where was Janet?      IN THE PLAY   IN THE AUDIENCE

**b** I thought that Janet was very interested in the play.
Where was Janet?      IN THE PLAY   IN THE AUDIENCE

**3 a** I must alter this dress before I wear it again.
Will I do the work myself?      YES   NO

**b** I must have this dress altered before I wear it again.
Will I do the work myself?      YES   NO

**4 a** 'Where's John?' 'He's gone walking.'
What kind of activity is this?      A SHORT ONE   A LONG ONE

**b** 'Where's John?' 'He's gone for a walk.'
What kind of activity is this?      A SHORT ONE   A LONG ONE

**5 a** You must have repaired the lawn mower.
Is the lawn mower still broken?      YES   NO

**b** You must have the lawn mower repaired.
Is the lawn mower still broken?      YES   NO

# 18 Phrasal verbs

▷ A phrasal verb is a compound, that is, it consists of a verb, eg *let*, and a particle, eg *down*, which together make a compound with a special meaning, eg *let down = disappoint*.

1  Choose one of the verbs below to fit each sentence:

**Verbs:** bring, fill, get, ~~let~~, make, put, put, run, take, turn, let

> Did Mark meet you at the airport?
>
> No, he __let__ me down, I had to get a train.

1  Did someone tell you that joke?

   No, I _____ it up.

2  Is there any mineral water left?

   No, we seem to have _____ out of it.

3  Did they accept your suggestion?

   No, they _____ it down.

4  Do you have somewhere I can sleep?

   No, but my sister has a spare room. She will _____ you up for the night.

5  I'd like to join the library.

   Please _____ this form out.

6  I can't stand pop music.

   I'm afraid you'll just have to _____ up with it.

7  Did the police catch the man who did it?

   No, he managed to _____ away.

8  What about the time you forgot my birthday?

   You promised not to _____ that subject up again.

9  You must be hot.

   I am. I think I'll _____ my pullover off.

10  Did John keep his promise?

   No, he _____ us down as usual.

71

## 2–3 Phrasal verbs

▷ When the object is a pronoun, it must come between the verb and the particle, eg *We have put it off*. In other cases, the object may come before or after the particle, eg *put the wedding off, put off the wedding*.

**2** Choose the right particle from the list to complete the sentences below. Make sure you also choose the correct form of the object pronoun:

Particles: away, away, back, down, down, off, off, out, up, up, up

> If cigarettes make you cough, give **them up**.

1  When you've finished with the newspaper, throw _____
2  If the radio's too loud for you, turn _____
3  If you don't know a word, look _____
4  If you don't need the lights on, switch _____
5  You can borrow my dictionary, but don't forget to give _____
6  If you haven't got an excuse, just make _____
7  Don't just throw your clothes anywhere: put _____ carefully.
8  Your voice is very loud: please keep _____
9  Those earrings look silly on you: take _____
10 You shouldn't smoke a cigarette in here: please put _____

**3** Now choose a verb and a particle to make sentences which mean the same as those below:

Verbs: call, carry, come, fall, grow, hold, set, sit, ~~stand~~, take, turn
Particles: back, down, off, off, on, on, out, round, ~~up~~, up, up

> On your feet, everybody!
> **Stand up!**

1  Please <u>continue</u>.
_____

2  You are welcome to <u>come to our house</u> any time.
_____

Phrasal verbs 3–4

3 He's on the other line. Please wait.
_____

4 What time did they finally arrive?
_____

5 I threw a boomerang last Wednesday, and it hasn't returned yet.
_____

6 What time do you intend to start your journey?
_____

7 Janet and Joe aren't talking to each other. They've had a quarrel.
_____

8 Please take a seat.
_____

▷ Sometimes a phrasal verb having the pattern verb + adverb is followed by a preposition, eg *run away from*.

**4** Choose an adverb and a preposition for each of the sentences below:

  Adverbs: away, down, out, in, up
Prepositions: for, from, of, on, with

> What might an unhappy child do?
> It might try to run __*away*__ __*from*__ home.

1 What does the newsagent say when he has no newspapers left?
  I'm sorry, we've sold _____ _____ newspapers.

2 What do you do if you have a low opinion of someone?
  You look _____ _____ him.

3 What do you do about a buzzing fly if you cannot catch it?
  You just have to put _____ _____ it.

4 What happens when a teacher is absent?
  Another teacher will stand _____ _____ her.

# 19 Adverbials

▷ Adverbials say something more about the manner, time or place of the action or state described by a verb, eg *She ran quickly. He left at five o'clock. They slept in a tent.* They also modify adjectives, eg *very good, not good enough.*

Adverbs of manner are usually formed by adding *-ly* to the adjective, eg *quick* → *quickly*. The ending *-ble* changes to *-bly*, eg *sensible* → *sensibly*. Most adjectives ending in *-ic* add *-ally*, eg *economic* → *economically*. There are a few special cases, eg *good* → *well, hard* → *hard.*

**1** Make adverbs from these adjectives:

| bad | badly |
|---|---|

1 happy _____
2 complete _____
3 useful _____
4 terrible _____
5 total _____
6 basic _____
7 useless _____
8 funny _____
9 equal _____
10 true _____

74

# Adverbials 2

**2** Choose a verb and make an adverb from the lists of adjectives below to fit each of the pictures:

  Verbs: breathe, listen, rain, run, share out, shine, sing, sleep, talk, wait, whisper

  Adjectives: bad, bright, careful, deep, equal, heavy, loud, patient, quick, soft, sound

She is running quickly.

1 _____
2 _____
3 _____
4 _____
5 _____
6 _____
7 _____
8 _____
9 _____
10 _____

## 3 Adverbials

**3** Write new sentences with a verb and an adverb:

> What can you say about someone who is a quiet speaker?
> He _speaks quietly._

What can you say about

1 someone who is a fast driver?

She _____

2 people who are heavy smokers?

They _____

3 someone who is a hard worker?

She _____

4 someone who is a fluent speaker?

He _____

5 someone who is a fluent speaker of French?

She _____

6 someone who is a good teacher?

He _____

7 people who are slow learners?

They _____

8 someone who is a careless driver?

She _____

# Adverbials 4

▷ Comparatives are formed with *more* + adverb, eg, *more quickly*. There are some special cases, eg *hard → harder*. Comparisons are also made with the construction *(not) as* adverb *as*, eg *She cannot run as quickly as I can*.

**4** Write a comparative for each of these sentences:

> Alice is a careful driver.
> She drives __*more carefully*__ than most people.

1 John is a heavy smoker.

   He smokes _____ than I do.

2 I am a fast driver.

   I drive _____ than everyone else.

3 She is a good teacher.

   She teaches _____ than most other teachers.

4 He is a bad teacher.

   He teaches _____ than most other teachers.

5 My children are slow learners.

   They learn _____ than many other students.

   They don't learn _____ as other students.

6 The Japanese are hard workers.

   They work _____ than we do.

   We don't work _____ as they do.

7 She is a good English teacher.

   She can speak _____ than I can.

   I can't speak _____ as she can.

## 5 Adverbials

▷ Word order is very important with adverbials. They may go at the beginning, eg *Frankly, I think she is mad*; in the middle, eg *He often tells lies*; or at the end, eg *We'll all meet again tomorrow*. If the adverb is put in another place, it is usually to give it emphasis, eg *Often, he tells lies; Tomorrow, we will all meet again.*

**5** Put the adverbials in their usual, non-emphatic position:

> He has gone out. (*just*)
> *He has just gone out.*

1 Have you finished your homework? (*yet*)

2 Have you seen an elephant fly? (*ever*)

3 Make sure you close the door. (*quietly*)

4 I don't think I have seen such a big one. (*ever*)

5 Tell me, does John work in a bank? (*still*)

6 We stay in bed late on Sundays. (*always*)

7 Don't be in such a hurry! Please eat your food! (*slowly*)

8 I'd lend you some money if I could. I haven't got any. (*unfortunately*)

9 I'm leaving you because I don't love you. (*any more*)

10 'Where's Janet?' 'She is in her study.' (*probably*)

# 20 Conjunctions

Conjunctions join words, phrases and sentences. Sometimes they are like simple links, eg *I knocked on the door and went in*; sometimes they show relationships in time, eg *I'll go when I'm ready*; in space, eg *Put it where there is room*; and others, eg *He looked as if he had seen a ghost*.

**1** Choose the correct conjunction for each of the sentences below:

**Conjunctions:** as far as, as soon as, ever since, just as, just before, until, when, wherever, while

> Finish your homework. Then you can go out.
>
> You can go out *as soon as you finish your homework.*

1 Finish your homework. Then you can go out.

   You cannot go out _____

2 He said goodbye to his children. Then he died.

   He said goodbye _____

3 I left school. I came to work in this bank.

   I've worked in this bank _____

4 Maria was cooking the dinner. We watched television.

   We watched television _____

5 We started to eat. The telephone rang.

   The telephone rang _____

6 Cigarettes used to cost sixpence a packet. I can remember that.

   I can remember _____

7 If I want to sit here, I will sit here.

   I'll sit _____

8 We could not go very far.

   We went _____

## 2 Conjunctions

**2** Combine these pairs of sentences using the words given in brackets. Make any other changes that are necessary.

> (*so late*)
> we went to bed     it was late
> *It was so late that we went to bed.*

(*so short that*)
1 he could not reach the top shelf     he was too short

(*even though*)
2 he was very short     he managed to reach the top shelf

(*such a cold day*)
3 we had to make a fire     it was a cold day

(*because*)
4 it was cold     we had to make a fire

(*so that he could*)
5 he wanted to buy a house     he saved up a lot of money

(*as long as*)
6 you can have a party     don't make a noise

(*in case*)
7 take your anoraks     it rains

(*as if*)
8 it might rain     it looks like it

## Conjunctions 3

**3** The conjunctions in this passage have got mixed up. Can you sort them out?

The other day, a man came into the shop THAT _____ we were closing. I was about to tell him we were closed WHETHER _____ he took out a pile of money SO _____ waved it under my nose. Obviously he was well off, JUST BECAUSE _____ he was dressed like a tramp, EVEN THOUGH _____ I decided to serve him.
'What can I do for you, sir?' I asked.
'I want to know JUST AS _____ you can repair my watch,' he said.
'I'm afraid we don't repair watches, sir,' I replied.
'Well, SO _____ you can't repair my watch, can you sell me a new one?'
IF _____ I told him that we didn't sell watches either, he became very angry.
'Well, your window is full of watches, WHEN _____ I naturally assumed you sold watches.'
'No, sir. AND _____ there are watches in the window, it doesn't mean that we sell them. Actually, we doctor cats.'
'Why have you got watches in the window, then?'
'We couldn't think what else to put in the window, sir.'

# 21 Reported speech

▷ Other people's words are reported using reporting verbs such as *say, tell, ask*. Reported speech makes some grammatical changes, eg *'Where are they?'* → *He asked me where they were; 'I'll do my best'* → *He says he will do his best.* Yes/no questions, when they are reported, are introduced by *if* or *whether*, eg *'Are you all right?'* → *He wants to know if we are all right*. With other questions, the question word is used, eg *'Why are you here?'* → *He wants to know why we are here*.

1 Rewrite these sentences in reported speech:

> 'Are you all right?'
>
> He wants to know *if we are all right*.

1 'Have you finished your homework?'

   He asked us _____

2 'Are you taking your children on holiday with you?'

   She wanted to know _____

3 'Is that your pen or mine?'

   Janet isn't sure _____

4 'Do you always wear your trousers back to front?'

   He wondered _____

5 'Can you speak without moving your lips?'

   He asked me _____

6 'Why have your books got "Rubbish" written on the front?'

   Mr Smith asked his pupils _____

7 'Where shall we meet this evening?'

   Alice would like to know _____

8 'Where shall we meet this evening?'

   Alice asked her friend _____

9 'Who wrote this word on the wall?'

   The police demanded to know _____

Reported speech    1–3

10 'Who were you talking to when I saw you?'

I want to know _____

**2** Study these sentences and then circle the right answer:

1 a She told us that Splaj is the capital of Threnodia?
   Is Splaj the capital of Threnodia?          YES   NO   DON'T KNOW
 b She told us that Splaj was the capital of Threnodia?
   Is Splaj the capital of Threnodia?          YES   NO   DON'T KNOW

2 a I wonder why nobody has arrived yet.
   Has anyone arrived yet?                     YES   NO   DON'T KNOW
 b I wonder if anybody has arrived yet.
   Has anyone arrived yet?                     YES   NO   DON'T KNOW

3 a The boss told his staff that they must work harder in future.
   When did he say this?                       RECENTLY   SOME TIME AGO
 b The boss told his staff they they had to work harder in future.
   When did he say this?                       RECENTLY   SOME TIME AGO

**3** What were the actual words used?

1 They told me that I should be more careful.

_____

2 They told me that I should have been more careful.

_____

3 Janet said that she didn't want to go.

_____

4 Janet said that she hadn't wanted to go.

_____

## 4 Reported speech

**4** Change the following conversation into reported speech:

'What's your name?'

'They call me the Camel-chaser.'

'What are you doing?'

'I'm putting white powder on the lawn.'

'Why are you putting white powder on the lawn?'

'I want to keep the camels away.'

'But there aren't any camels around here!'

'I know. It's very good powder.'

'Are you crazy?'

'I may be crazy, but I don't have any camels in my garden.'

---

1 First she asked him _____ _____

2 He told her that _____ _____

3 She wanted to know _____ _____

4 He replied that _____ _____

5 Then she asked him _____ _____

6 He explained that _____ _____

7 She pointed out that _____ _____

8 He told her that _____, and that _____ powder.

9 She asked him then _____ _____

10 He replied that _____ and that _____ garden.

# Answer Key

## 1 Nouns

**1**

1 leaf  2 halves  3 woman  4 goose
5 deer  6 kilos  7 bus  8 countries
9 holidays  10 tooth  11 box
12 thieves  13 toe  14 books  15 fly
16 coaches

**2**

1 is  2 are  3 Does  4 looks  5 Is
6 have  7 need  8 makes  9 tell
10 is

**3**

1 I need two tomatoes and three potatoes.
2 A knife is used to cut things.
3 Are those your babies?
4 Let's make some bookshelves.
5 My teeth hurt: please take them out.
6 These women are housewives.
7 This is my grandchild (or 'grandson' or 'granddaughter').
8 Here are some photos of my daughter.
9 There were some sheep in the garden.
10 This shoe is too tight for my foot.

**4**

1 niece  2 uncle  3 actress
4 husband  5 granddaughter
6 lord or gentleman  7 widower
8 policewoman  9 prince
10 mistress  11 heroine  12 girlfriend
13 bridegroom  14 waitress  15 cow
16 king

**5**

1 male: his  2 female: her
3 don't know  4 female: her
5 don't know  6 female: niece
7 don't know  8 male: he
9 don't know
10 male: Mary's husband

**6**

1 matchstick  2 wristwatch
3 post office  4 airport
5 washing machine  6 armchair
7 bottle opener  8 greenhouse
9 screwdriver  10 telephone booth

**7**

1 three weeks' wages
2 yesterday's problems
3 in three years' time
4 in a few minutes' time
5 John's books
6 the children's room
7 the Smiths' house
8 Mr Jones' secretary (People also say 'Mr Jones's secretary because it is easier to pronounce)
9 the men's room
10 the girls' study
11 at the greengrocer's
12 at the optician's
13 to the dentist's
14 at/from the chemist's
15 At the baker's (or At the bakery)

## 2 Determiners I

**1**

1 I'm wearing a yellow shirt and an orange tie.
2 An honest man is a happy man.
3 This is an easy exercise.
4 Is there a university in your town?
5 He is paid a pound an hour for his work.
6 A hammer is a useful tool.
7 'An apple a day keeps the doctor away.'

**2**

1 Which animals make the best pets, cats or dogs?
2 How do you like your coffee?
3 With cream and brown sugar.
4 Is bullfighting the most popular sport in Spain?
5 It is popular, especially with tourists (or the tourists), but the sport that most Spaniards enjoy is football.
6 On Saturdays, we usually have dinner early and then go to the cinema.
7 My wife and I go to church on Sunday morning, except when the children are on holiday.
8 Do you go to school on foot?
9 No, we usually go on the bus. (Note that we say 'by' + means of transport,' except horse and bicycle, eg 'by bus' but 'on/in the' when referring to a particular vehicle, eg we went on the bus, we went in the car)
10 How do you start this car? Put the key in the ignition, and turn it. Put your foot on the accelerator, and, as long as there is petrol (or some petrol) in the tank, it should start.

**3**

1 This is a picture of a/the house where I lived when I was a child.
2 French people shake hands more often than the English do.
3 Let me give you a piece of advice.
4 Do you know the difference between Great Britain and the United Kingdom?
5 I know that Britain is not the same thing as the British Isles.
6 The trouble with old furniture is that it is too big for modern houses.
7 The Earth goes round the Sun.
8 Have you got a library in your school? Yes, and the teacher in charge of it says that most of the books are out of date.
9 'The best things in life are free.' (proverb)

**4**

1 take place  2 made friends
3 make fun  4 take care  5 catch cold
6 pay attention  7 have time
8 changing jobs

**5**

John is a very good friend of mine. He is a bus driver and his wife is a waitress. They live in a small house in the centre of a village. The house has two bedrooms and a small garden at the back. They have two children, the younger is a boy, the older is a girl. Because the house is so small, the children have to share a bedroom, but this is not a problem because they are still very young. They go to the same school. Because it is not far from the house where they live, they usually go to school on foot except when the weather is very bad. Then they take the bus.

**6**

1 This is a screwdriver, that is a spanner.
2 These are screws and those are nuts and bolts.
3 This is a cat and those are mice.
4 These are cakes and that is a loaf of bread.
5 This is a typewriter, that is a computer.

## 3 Determiners II

**1**

1 some, any
2 any ('some' only if you expect the answer 'yes')
3 anything
4 some (ie, you are inviting him. Use 'any' if you simply wish to ask a question)
5 any
6 Nobody

85

# Answer key

7 anyone ('someone' only if you expect the answer 'yes')
8 anything ('something' only if you wish to suggest that you are expecting them to drop something)
9 None
10 Somebody

**2**

1 much, a few  2 much
3 much, a little  4 a few  5 much
6 much  7 much, much  8 much
9 many  10 a little

**3**

| | | |
|---|---|---|
| 1 I can see | | some schoolgirls |
| 2 There are some | | some dogs |
| 3 | | some cars |
| 4 | | some shops |
| there aren't | any schoolboys. | |
| but I can't see | any cats. | |
| there are no | buses. | |
| | churches. | |

**4**

1 a few minutes
2 a notebook/Have you got one?
3 Here is some information about Indonesia.
4 How many days/Not many.
5 some more coal
6 a few bottles of orange juice/not many cartons of milk
7 some tobacco/some
8 Was there much traffic in town?
9 This is my luggage. Where shall I put it?

## 4 Determiners III

**1**

1 both of them/either of them
2 all of them/any of them
3 Let's all go
4 every one of them
5 all the children/each one
6 20 pence each
7 all my teachers/each
8 either
9 Tell them all
10 either of them

**2**

1 both of them, them both
2 Both of us, We both
3 All of them, They all
4 All of them would, They would all
5 all of us, us all

**3**

1 So have I  2 Neither can I
3 Neither do I  4 So would I
5 So do I  6 So am I
7 Neither will I *or* Neither shall I
8 Neither did I

## 5 Adjectivals

**1**

tall: has got a child with her and she is carrying a shopping basket.
tall: has got a child with her but she is not carrying a shopping basket.
short: has got a child with her and she is carrying a shopping basket.
short: hasn't got a child with her, but she is carrying a shopping basket.

**2**

fat: he isn't wearing a hat/hasn't got a hat on, and he's standing next to a car.
fat: he's wearing a hat/has got a hat on, and he's standing next to a lamp post.
thin: he isn't wearing a hat/hasn't got a hat on and he's standing next to a car.
thin: he's wearing a hat/has got a hat on and he's standing next to a lamp post.

**3**

1 all my old school photographs
2 all our other German friends
3 all of the last six indoor meetings
4 most of her next five television shows
5 half of these other green peppers
6 a pretty little grey-haired French lady
7 two famous old landscape paintings
8 this interesting oval-shaped Victorian mirror
9 a beautiful young Arab racehorse
10 a great big black and white sheepdog

**4**

| | | |
|---|---|---|
| 1 big | bigger | biggest |
| 2 easy | easier | easiest |
| 3 sad | sadder | saddest |
| 4 early | earlier | earliest |
| 5 flat | flatter | flattest |
| 6 heavy | heavier | heaviest |
| 7 clean | cleaner | cleanest |
| 8 grey | greyer | greyest |
| 9 common | commoner | commonest |
| 10 fat | fatter | fattest |
| 11 quiet | quieter | quietest |
| 12 far | farther | farthest |
| far | further | furthest |
| 13 narrow | narrower | narrowest |
| 14 thin | thinner | thinnest |
| 15 sunny | sunnier | sunniest |
| 16 ill/bad | worse | worst |

**5**

1 Air is lighter than water.
2 I find maths less difficult than physics.
3 Water is not as light as air.
4 A metre is longer than a yard.
5 Stealing is worse than telling lies.
6 Pluto is more distant than Mars.
7 My father is not as old as my mother.
8 Fish are commoner/more common than whales.

**6**

1 It's the tastiest steak I have ever eaten.
2 It's the fastest car I have ever driven.
3 He's the cleverest man I have ever spoken to.
4 This is the worst beer I have ever drunk.
5 She is the quietest woman/girl/person I have ever met.

**7**

1 fell asleep  2 come true
3 get better  4 go mad  5 growing old
6 keep quiet  7 sit still  8 make sure
9 turned blue

**8**

| | | My nationality |
|---|---|---|
| *I am from* | *I am a(n)* | *is* |
| 1 Canada | Canadian | Canadian |
| 2 Spain | Spaniard | Spanish |
| 3 Russia | Russian | Russian |
| 4 Germany | German | German |
| 5 Turkey | Turk | Turkish |
| 6 Finland | Finn | Finnish |
| 7 Greece | Greek | Greek |
| 8 USA | American | American |
| 9 Poland | Pole | Polish |
| 10 Denmark | Dane | Danish |
| 11 Sweden | Swede | Swedish |
| 12 Italy | Italian | Italian |
| 13 Scotland | Scot | Scottish |
| 14 Portugal | Portuguese | Portuguese |
| 15 Switzerland | Swiss | Swiss |
| 16 Peru | Peruvian | Peruvian |
| 17 Japan | Japanese | Japanese |
| 18 Brazil | Brazilian | Brazilian |
| 19 Thailand | Thai | Thai |
| 20 Israel | Israeli | Israeli |

**9**

1 seventy-nine
2 three hundred and sixty-five

# Answer key

3 one thousand five hundred and forty-two
4 four thousand and fifty
5 fourteen thousand five hundred
6 a/one hundred thousand
7 two hundred and three thousand six hundred and fifty-four
8 one million three hundred and thirty thousand
9 (nought) point seven five
10 three point seven six
11 oh one three seven oh double two double nine
12 oh five two six double oh two seven double oh
13 the twelfth of April/April the twelfth, nineteen eighty-nine
14 the fourteenth of August/August the fourteenth, nineteen ninety-two
15 the twenty-third of May/May the twenty-third, ten sixty-six

## 6 Pronouns

**1**

| I | me | my | mine | myself |
|---|---|---|---|---|
| we | us | our | ours | ourselves |
| you | you | your | yours | yourself |
| you | you | your | yours | yourselves |
| he | him | his | his | himself |
| she | her | her | hers | herself |
| they | them | their | theirs | themselves |
| it | it | its | its | itself |

**2**

1 his shirts himself
2 she loves them both
3 keep it to yourself
4 their umbrellas with them
5 hurt themselves
6 with us. We all enjoyed ourselves
7 for you, made it all by myself
8 which are his and which are hers

**3**

1 It's four o'clock.
2 It's raining.
3 It's the tenth of June.
4 It's me!
5 It's going to rain.
   It looks like rain.
6 It's difficult to understand what he says.
7 It's hard to bring up a child on your own.
8 It isn't easy to learn without a teacher.
9 It's useful to know foreign languages.
10 It's funny to see yourself on video.
11 It's a pity to say goodnight.
12 It's no use crying over spilt milk. (proverb)

**4**

1 There's a sheep on the roof.
2 There are two cats looking out of an upstairs window.
3 There's a horse on the chimney.
4 There are three dogs up the tree.
5 There's an elephant behind the house.
6 There's an old man with a beard standing in the doorway.
7 There's an old woman leaning out of a downstairs window.
8 There are a lot of children.

**5**

1 mine
2 my/myself
3 one/the other/yourself
4 mine
5 one another
6 it to me
7 She
8 others/white
9 his

## 7 Prepositions

**1**

up the steps, under the bridge, through the park, down the hill, along the river, over the gate, into the bank.

**2**

1 at  2 since  3 for  4 at
5 until/before  6 until  7 by
8 after/past

**3**

1 for  2 of  3 at  4 in  5 on  6 of
7 with  8 to  9 about  10 from

**4**

1 looked everywhere for  2 look after
3 longing for  4 apologise for
5 depend on  6 believe in
7 thank you for  8 congratulated her on
9 borrow money from, lend money to
10 prevent it from  11 suffer from
12 takes after

**5**

1 on purpose  2 by heart
3 out of order  4 at home
5 for my sake  6 by sight  7 for good
8 in vain  9 on time

**6**

1 According to  2 in spite of
3 except (for)/apart from  4 instead of
5 apart from/except for

## 8 Introduction to verbs

**1**

| 1 choose | chose | chosen |
|---|---|---|
| 2 feel | felt | felt |
| 3 put | put | put |
| 4 pay | paid | paid |
| 5 grow | grew | grown |
| 6 call | called | called |
| 7 give | gave | given |
| 8 seem | seemed | seemed |
| 9 lose | lost | lost |
| 10 sell | sold | sold |
| 11 beat | beat | beaten |
| 12 tell | told | told |
| 13 catch | caught | caught |
| 14 become | became | become |
| 15 keep | kept | kept |
| 16 fall | fell | fallen |
| 17 cost | cost | cost |
| 18 eat | ate | eaten |
| 19 drive | drove | driven |
| 20 show | showed | shown |

**2**

1 think: think thought thought
2 teach: teach taught taught
3 wear: wear wore worn
4 stand: stand stood stood
5 shoot: shoot shot shot
6 say: say said said

**3**

1 He drew a picture.
2 He found a mistake.
3 He forgot his key.
4 He lit a cigarette.
5 He made a mistake.
6 He sent her a letter.
7 He tore his shirt on a nail.
8 He wrote a very good essay.

**4**

1 I have drawn a picture.
2 I have found a mistake.
3 I have forgotten my key.
4 I have lit a cigarette.
5 I have made a mistake.
6 I have sent a letter to her/sent her a letter.
7 I have torn my shirt on a nail.
8 I have written an essay.

**5**

1 come  2 hidden  3 left, left
4 went, met  5 stuck  6 held
7 forgiven  8 meant, sat  9 run
10 slept

**6**

1 Did she get  2 Do you study
3 Did you hear  4 Are your students

87

# Answer key

5 Have the others read
6 Will her brother be away
7 Did you ring   8 Do you want

**7**

1 we didn't go out
2 he can't/cannot play   3 I didn't do
4 I didn't win   5 I won't/will not cut
6 he didn't shake   7 I haven't got
8 he doesn't speak

**8**

1 didn't you?   2 aren't they?
3 mustn't we?   4 won't we?
5 can't you?   6 wouldn't you?
7 shall we?   8 isn't he?   9 hasn't he?
10 haven't we?

**9**

1 No, I can't   2 No, they haven't
3 No, we haven't   4 No, I/we couldn't
5 No, they weren't   6 No, he won't
7 No, they didn't   8 No, I'm not

## 9 Simple and continuous tenses

**1**

1 The policeman is standing on his hands.
2 The doctor isn't wearing any shoes.
3 The sailor is looking through the wrong end of a telescope.
4 The roadsweeper is holding his broom upside down.
5 Policemen direct traffic.
6 Doctors look after people who are ill.
7 Sailors go to sea.
8 Roadsweepers keep the roads clean.

**2**

1 When do you get paid?
2 What are you doing this evening?
3 When did you leave school?
4 When/How often do you go shopping?
5 What did you do last night?
6 Where were you going when I saw you?
7 When did you get married?
8 What is your daughter doing?
9 How many/What/Which languages do you speak?
10 How did you hurt yourself?

**3**

1 The man is weighing himself.
  The meat weighs two kilos.
2 The Smiths have/have got a new car.
  They are having dinner.
3 The waiter is smelling the wine.
  The wine smells terrible!
4 This petrol can holds one/a gallon.

The little girl is holding some (a bunch of) flowers.
5 Mother is taking the children to school.
  This parking meter takes twenty pence coins.

**4**

1 a yes
1 b no
2 a no
2 b yes
3 a yes
3 b no
4 a no
4 b yes
5 a yes
5 b no

**5**

1 will leave/leaves/is leaving
2 used to be/was once
3 Are you coming
4 sit
5 have/have got
6 I'll be working/I'm working

## 10 Perfect tenses

**1**

1 She has fallen off her bicycle.
2 He has broken his glasses.
3 He has dropped his shopping basket.
4 A dog has bitten him and torn his trousers.
5 A lorry has gone through the shop window.
6 A thief has stolen the wheels from the car.

**2**

1 There was a girl who had fallen off her bicycle.
2 There was a man who had broken his glasses.
3 There was a man who had dropped his shopping basket.
4 There was a policeman who had torn his trousers.
5 There was a lorry which had gone through a shop window.
6 There was a thief who had stolen some car wheels.

**3**

1 The girl is tired because she has been working too hard.
2 The little boy is coughing because he has been smoking (one of) his father's cigars.
3 The boys are wet because they have been swimming in the lake.

4 The man is angry because he has been waiting for ages.
5 The roads are wet because it has been raining.

**4**

1 The girl was tired because she had been working too hard.
2 The little boy was coughing because he had been smoking (one of) his father's cigars.
3 The boys were wet because they had been swimming in the lake.
4 The man was angry because he had been waiting for ages.
5 The roads were wet because it had been raining.

**5**

1 I did not go out at all last week.
2 I haven't been out much recently.
3 I've done a lot of work during the last few days.
4 I haven't played football since I was at school.
5 I haven't been able to do much work lately.
6 I went swimming a lot when I was at school.

## 11 The future

**1**

1 A: don't
  B: is/will be closed
  A: we'll go
2 A: Will you come
  A: I'll see
3 A: Will you be coming
  B: I'll come/doesn't finish
  A: will finish
4 A: Will you help
  B: I'm taking

**2**

1 A: is going to rain
  B: are you doing
  A: is/shall go
  B: I'll come
2 A: add
  B: get
  A: put
  B: will have
3 A: I'll be/I've finished
  B: shan't be
4 A: is going to be/sees
  B: won't even notice

**3**

Suggested answers:
1 He's going to fall off his bike if he's not careful!

# Answer key

2 She's going to cut herself if she doesn't watch out.
3 Look out, you're going to run over that dog if you're not careful!
4 The taxidriver's going to have an accident if he's not careful.
5 The waiter's going to spill the wine any second now!
6 Those two men are going to start fighting in a minute!

**4**

1 finishes/has finished
2 send for you
3 tells us to
4 starts to rain
5 has run/runs
6 don't want to
7 have had
8 asks me

## 12 Modals

**1**

1 will have to
2 having to
3 have had to
4 having to
5 won't have to
6 will/shall have to
7 having to/going to have to
8 must/have to
9 had to
10 had had to

**2**

1 couldn't/wasn't able to
2 won't be able to
3 could have/would have been able to
4 Have you been able to
5 can't
6 can/could
7 be able to
8 be able to
9 could have
10 couldn't/wasn't able to

**3**

1 have to   2 be able to   3 be able to
4 have to   5 to be able to   6 had to
7 have to   8 have had to

**4**

1 can't be   2 must be
3 can't be   4 could be/might be
5 can't be/couldn't be
6 must be/could be   7 must be
8 can't be/couldn't be
9 can be/could be
10 must be

**5**

1 a an order
1 b a piece of advice
2 a obliged not to
2 b not obliged to
3 a stating a fact
3 b making a guess
4 a before ten
4 b after ten
5 a yes
5 b don't know
6 a a piece of advice
6 b an order
7 a a certainty
7 b a probability

## 13 Conditionals

**1**

Suggested answers
1 If you throw a lighted match into the
   or   threw
   petrol, you will   cause an explosion.
                      would
2 If you play   with knives,
   or   played
   you will   cut yourself.
              would
3 If you take these pills,
   or   took
   you will   feel better.
              would
4 If you ask   me to dance,
   or   asked
   I will/might   say 'Yes'.
   would/might
5 If you pull   the lion's tail,
   or   pulled
   he might eat you.
         might
6 If you save   your money,
   or   saved
   you will   be able to buy a house.
              would
7 If you practise   hard,
   or   practised
   you could become a concert pianist.
                     could
8 If you study hard
   or   studied
   you should get a degree.
              should

**2**

1 could/would get
2 could/would earn
3 he earned, could/would buy
4 had/had bought, could/would get
5 could have/would have
6 would need
7 needed, have to get/find
8 studied
9 became
10 was/were, would have

11 would be very poor/would suffer, etc
12 would be

**3**

1 a don't know
1 b no
2 a no
2 b yes
3 a no
3 b yes
4 a wet
4 b fine
5 a no
5 b don't know

## 14 The passive

**1**

1 are not allowed
2 is dedicated
3 are being built/were built/have been built
4 will be given/is to be given
5 has not yet been reached
6 was planted
7 will be awarded
  be sent in
8 must be kept

**2**

1 I was shown
2 We were being shown
3 You will now be told
4 I want to be told
5 These students are being taught
6 They have been asked
7 You might be sent
8 He is not allowed to

**3**

Suggested answers:
1 This machine does not/will not give change.
2 This is a shop where you can buy and sell books.
3 If your washing machine has broken down, we can repair it for you.
4 We clear rubbish/will clear your rubbish.
5 You are not allowed to/You must not smoke in the corridors.
6 If you are not satisfied, we will return your money/give you your money back.
7 Before you buy a car from us, we check it and test it.
8 This club does not admit children under 16.

# Answer key

## 15 The imperative

**1**

1 j  2 c  3 i  4 k  5 b
6 d  7 g  8 e  9 a  10 h  11 f

**2**

Suggested answers:
1 Let's stay in and watch TV.
2 Let's have something to eat.
3 Let's go to bed.
4 Let's do it together.
5 Let's have/go to a party.

**3**

1 Don't let Susan pick the flowers.
2 Let Joe drive the car.
3 Don't let the thief get away.
4 Let the children play football.
5 Don't let the fire go out.

**4**

Suggested answers:
1 Would you be quiet, please?
2 Will you put your books away, please?
3 Would you mind telling me what you're doing?
4 Could you help me with these suitcases, please?
5 Would you mind/Do you mind not doing that?
6 Would you please keep your dog under control?
7 Will you leave me alone, please?
8 Could you hurry up please?
9 Would you mind passing the salt, please?
10 Would you mind not making so much noise?

## 16 Gerund and infinitive

**1**

Suggested answers:
1 (has) succeeded in lifting
2 is used to writing
3 hasn't managed to get
4 he is refusing/has refused to eat
5 good at telling
6 is thinking/has been thinking of going
7 promises/has promised to be
8 keeps (on) making
9 have agreed to ban
10 avoid eating

**2**

1 I can't help biting my fingernails.
2 I don't mind doing a lot of homework.
3 I hope to finish this essay.
4 I don't remember lending you a fiver.
5 I've never tried swimming.
6 I didn't expect to see you here.
7 I shall not bother to reply/replying.
8 I dislike being/having to be nice.
9 I believe in looking after myself.
10 I cannot afford to get/buy a new car.

**3**

1 to try  2 to seeing  3 go
4 drinking  5 me to believe  6 to go
7 you telling  8 making, laugh
9 if I close  10 to post

**4**

1 a Yes
  b No
2 a Yes
  b Don't know
3 a No
  b Yes

## 17 Participles

**1**

1 going dancing
2 went swimming
3 are going windsurfing
4 We'll go climbing
5 has gone skiing
6 going horse riding
7 took me fishing
8 would have gone bowling

**2**

1 need mending
2 need pressing/ironing
3 needs cutting
4 need throwing away
5 needs tidying up
6 need washing
7 needs repairing
8 need feeding

**3**

Suggested answers:
1 I'm going to have/get it repaired.
2 I had/got it fixed.
3 I ought to get it repaired/have it seen to.
4 Well, you could always have it altered.
5 I know, I'm going to get/have it cut.
6 You ought to have them tested.

**4**

1 a well-dressed man
2 an exciting adventure
3 a knitted pullover
4 a terrifying experience
5 a broken promise
6 home-made jam
7 a disappointing performance
8 a curved line
9 a new-laid egg
10 bored children

**5**

1 a no
1 b yes
2 a in the play
2 b in the audience
3 a yes
3 b no
4 a a long one
4 b a short one
5 a no
5 b yes

## 18 Phrasal verbs

**1**

1 made  2 run  3 turned  4 put
5 fill  6 put  7 get  8 bring  9 take
10 let

**2**

1 it away  2 it down  3 it up
4 them off  5 it back  6 one up
7 them away  8 it down  9 them off
10 it out

**3**

1 carry on  2 call round  3 hold on
4 turn up  5 come back  6 set off
7 fallen out  8 sit down

**4**

1 out of  2 down on  3 up with
4 in for

## 19 Adverbials

**1**

1 happily  2 completely  3 usefully
4 terribly  5 totally  6 basically
7 uselessly  8 funnily  9 equally
10 truly

**2**

Suggested answers:
1 The child is sleeping soundly.
2 The people are talking loudly.
3 The man is listening carefully.
4 The queue is waiting patiently.
5 The sun is shining brightly.

# Answer key

6 Two lovers are whispering softly.
7 It is raining heavily.
8 She is breathing deeply.
9 The children are sharing the cake out equally.
10 The woman is singing badly.

**3**
1 She drives fast.
2 They smoke heavily.
3 She works hard.
4 He speaks fluently.
5 She speaks French fluently.
6 He teaches well.
7 They learn slowly.
8 She drives carelessly.

**4**
1 He smokes more heavily
2 I drive faster
3 She teaches better
4 He teaches worse
5 They learn more slowly
   They don't learn as/so quickly
6 They work harder
   We don't work as hards
7 She can speak English better
   I can't speak English as/so well

**5**
1 Have you finished your homework yet?
2 Have you ever seen an elephant fly?
3 Make sure you close the door quietly.
4 I don't think I have ever seen such a big one.
5 Tell me, does John still work in a bank?
6 We always stay in bed late on Sundays.
7 Don't be in such a hurry! Please eat your food slowly.
8 Unfortunately, I haven't got any/I haven't got any, unfortunately.
9 I'm leaving you because I don't love you any more.
10 Janet is probably in her study.

## 20  Conjunctions

**1**
Suggested answers:
1 You cannot go out until you finish/have finished your homework.
2 He said goodbye to his children just before he died.
3 I've worked in this bank ever since I left school.
4 We watched television while Maria cooked/was cooking the dinner.
5 The telephone rang just as we started to eat.

6 I can remember when cigarettes used to cost . . .
7 I'll sit wherever I want to/like.
8 We went as far as we could.

**2**
Suggested answers:
1 He was so short that he could not reach the top shelf.
2 He managed to reach the top shelf even though he was very short.
3 It was such a cold day that we had to make a fire.
4 Because it was so cold, we had to make a fire.
*or* We had to make a fire because it was so cold.
5 He saved up a lot of money so that he could buy a house.
6 You can have a party as long as you don't make a noise.
7 Take your anoraks in case it rains.
8 It looks as if it might rain.

**3**
The other day, a man came into the shop JUST AS we were closing. I was about to tell him we were closed WHEN he took out a pile of money AND waved it under my nose. Obviously he was well off, EVEN THOUGH he was dressed like a tramp, AND I decided to serve him.
'What can I do for you, sir?' I asked.
'I want to know WHETHER you can repair my watch,' he said.
'I'm afraid we don't repair watches, sir,' I replied.
'Well, IF you can't repair my watch, can you sell me a new one?'
WHEN I told him that we didn't sell watches either, he became very angry.
'Well, your window is full of watches, SO I naturally assumed you sold watches.'
'No, sir. JUST BECAUSE there are watches in the window, it doesn't mean that we sell them. Actually, we doctor cats.'
'Why have you got watches in the window, then?'
'We couldn't think what else to put in the window, sir.'

## 21  Reported speech

**1**
Suggested answers:
1 He asked us if/whether we had finished our homework.
2 She wanted to know if/whether we were taking our children on holiday with us.

3 Janet isn't sure if/whether this is my pen or hers.
4 He wondered if/whether I always wore/wear my trousers back to front.
5 He asked me if/whether I could speak without moving my lips.
6 Mr Smith asked his pupils why their books had (got) 'Rubbish' written on the front.
7 Alice would like to know where we shall/will/should meet this evening.
8 Alice asked her friend where they would/should meet that evening.
9 The police demanded to know who had written that word on the wall.
10 I want to know who you were talking to when I saw you.

**2**
1 a  yes
1 b  don't know
2 a  no
2 b  don't know
3 a  recently
3 b  some time ago

**3**
1 'You should be more careful'
2 'You should have been more careful'
3 'I don't want to go'
4 'I didn't want to go'

**4**
1 First she asked him his name/what his name was.
2 He told her that they called him/his name was the Camel-chaser.
3 She wanted to know what he was doing.
4 He replied that he was putting white powder on the lawn.
5 Then she asked him why he was putting . . .
6 He explained that he wanted to keep . . .
7 She pointed out that there weren't any camels around there.
8 He told her that he knew, . . . and that it was very good powder.
9 She asked him then if he was crazy.
10 He replied that he might be crazy, but that he didn't have any camels in his garden.